MAKE A SIGNAL

MAKE A SIGNAL

Captain Jack Broome
DSC RN

ILLUSTRATED BY THE AUTHOR

DOUGLAS - BOYD BOOKS

First published July 1955 by Putnam London.
This edition published October1994
by Douglas - Boyd Books
Stream Cottage, Scrag Oak, Wadhurst
East Sussex TN5 6NP

Distributed by Maritime Books
Lodge Hill
Liskeard
Cornwall PL14 4EL

A CIP record for this book is available from the British Library.
ISBN 0 9514480 1 3

Printed in Great Britain by Antony Rowe Ltd. Chippenham.

CONTENTS

5

PREFACE

This is a book about naval signals. A signal is a sign which conveys information. When ships first found themselves beyond shouting range the language of naval signals was born.

In the beginning this language was expressed by the positions, colours and meanings of flags and banners. The more manœuvrable and co-operative ships became the more the language expanded, until it reached its most colourful peak in the early part of this century. But now it is changing altogether. Soon, the very word signal will be obsolete, for signs are no longer needed to convey information. Today, information is poured, irrespective of distance, from brain to brain. The air is saturated with it. One day it will condense and, paradoxically, form fog.

This book is concerned mainly with the pre-microphone period; with signals that travel alone and, like telegrams, have to be carefully worded to be readily understood. Unlike telegrams, however, they are impersonal and public. They carry the authority of a ship or a squadron. They are paid for with reputations, sometimes even with human lives.

The era of such signals produced craftsmen who could compose on a pad the exact phrase to suit the situation. Their signals had power and penetration; they inspired, provoked, amused or debunked with an aptitude all their own. A signal at sea which commended was round the ship like a flash of light. One which reproved spread gloom just as quickly.

A signal records the immediate reaction of the man-on-the-spot; a recorded sequence of them gives a lively impression of the incident it covers. To illustrate this I have taken several operations and incidents—most of which are already well known

7

—and reconstructed them on the framework of the signals which conducted them.

I have also included some signals which, in themselves, have undoubtedly influenced the course of history; though to what extent must remain in doubt. But for that primitive signal in 480 B.C., what would have happened to the Greeks in the Battle of Salamis? How much more effort did Nelson wring from those under his command by his famous signal at Trafalgar? How many ships did the Admiralty's signals to Russian Convoy P.Q.17 cost?

Last in the book is a collection of individual signals. Some are seasoned chestnuts; but a few, I hope, are new. It seems the moment now to harvest them, at the end of this era of conciseness. One cannot imagine such pithy exchanges as some of those between Admirals Somerville and Cunningham, being spoken on radio telephone.

When I began to make this collection, I did not think it would be very difficult—just a matter of skimming through old signal logs and drawing off the cream. I went first to Mr Ellmers, of Admiralty Records, and explained my object. Casually, I asked how many signals had been sent in the Royal Navy during World War II. His reply was: "About two hundred tons."

Mr Ellmers' department is highly efficient. Provided one knows when, where and by whom a signal was made, his team will delve into that great signal rick and emerge in a remarkably short time, dusty but triumphant, with what one is seeking. Unfortunately, in many cases I was not at all sure what I was seeking until I saw it. The only other source of supply was living memory; and I would like here to express my sincere gratitude to all those—from Sea Lord to Signal Bos'n—who have taken the trouble to search their memories and send me the result.

Since this book is mostly concerned with the text of signals, no attempt has been made to introduce personalities which are not already well known. The same applies to technicalities; even latitudes and longitudes are omitted. To some signals there are several different versions. If the wrong one appears, I apologise; living memory is not always strictly accurate. There was, you may recall, the case of Nelson's great friend, Captain the Hon. Henry Blackwood, who commanded H.M.S. *Euryalus* at Trafalgar. In a letter written the day after the battle he quoted Nelson's famous signal as:

ENGLAND EXPECTS EVERY OFFICER AND MAN WILL DO THEIR UTMOST DUTY.

And even Admiral Collingwood, Nelson's second-in-command, had a ring inscribed with the words:

ENGLAND EXPECTS EVERYTHING: MEN DO YOUR DUTY.

From Age to Age

Once upon a time, our forefathers decided to ease themselves down from the trees they lived in and become human beings. Having made this decision, the operation must have been planned. Some particular forefather must have been in charge. By grunt or by gesture someone must have given the signal.

This means of intercommunication had limitations. Probably, at the conferences which followed, one particular forefather was told to look into the matter and draw up some improvements. The matter has been under review ever since.

Even in those days there was plenty of material to work on. The possibilities of signalling by sound were suggested by the trumpeting of the mighty Mastodon. Our forefathers soon found they could tell whether he was seeking a meal or a mate. The reflection of the sun from wet pebbles was noted. Smoke by day and fires by night were suitable for spreading a warning. In the Old Testament Jeremiah called upon his people to "set up a sign of fire . . . for evil appeareth to the North, and Great Destruction."

Some forefathers felt the call of the sea as soon as they reached the ground. It drew them out to the coasts with that force which still prevails on Bank Holidays, and there they stayed.

They learnt to swim, but found they could not live in the water. It was too cold. They preferred to keep warm and dry. This gave them a lively interest in anything which floated, especially if it would support them. The first forefather to catch and fry a fish added to this interest.

Having launched the shipbuilding industry they soon found it necessary to identify their craft. People were suspicious in those days. Everyone was a potential disturber of everyone else's peace until he could prove himself otherwise. Individuals and communities were therefore identified by their standards. A standard in this, its earliest sense, was a tall pole supporting some distinctive object. A shipowner took his standard to sea with him. Designs on pottery made by the pre-dynastic Egyptians as far back as 4000 B.C. show what is believed to be boats, used on the Nile at that time, with the standard mounted on the aftermost cabin.

For the next three and a half thousand years there seem to have been matters more pressing to attend to than the development of signalling. Then, in 480 B.C., came the first record of an operational signal made between ships at sea.

It happened during the battle of Salamis. As this signal was the ancestor of all the others in this book, the story is told in full. Xerxes, the Persian ruler, had spent four years raising an army to overthrow the Greeks. The force he raised was not a happy army, but it was the biggest the world had yet seen. At the outset of the campaign Xerxes was unopposed. The smaller Greek states showed no national patriotism. Athens became alarmed and sent Themistocles, the best leader they could find. He managed to raise some opposition, and it was largely due to his counsel and energy that the Greeks were not completely overwhelmed.

But Xerxes and his hordes swept on. When he reached the Dardanelles he built a bridge of boats, crossed over, and turned down the coast towards Greece. Offshore a fleet of miscellaneous ships backed him up with supplies.

At the pass of Thermopylae, the gateway to Athens, the Persians found 1,400 Spartans under the leadership of Leonidas blocking their path. After fighting with great heroism every single one of this gallant little army was killed; but they left their mark on the Persians, and it was in a chastened mood that they entered Athens.

At this stage it seemed to Xerxes that he had achieved his object and conquered Greece. But he had not reckoned with the Greek navy.

This small fleet was lying off Salamis. When the grim news came through from Athens, there was disagreement between the Commanders. Some favoured retirement to the Isthmus of Corinth, but Themistocles, who was still very much alive, urged battle with the Persian supply fleet. He let it be known that the Greeks intended to withdraw, which enticed the Persians to give chase. When the two fleets met, the Greeks were outnumbered by four to one. But they soon proved that they were craftier than their pursuers.

Having formed into an orthodox line of battle, the Persians looked as if they were going to have it all their own way. But, suddenly, the scene changed. In the Greek flagship an oar was raised. Attached to the oar was a red cloak. The moment it appeared the Greek ships swung round together and bore down upon their adversaries who were soon in complete confusion.

The Greek victory which followed relieved the threat to European civilisation. The first manœuvring signal at sea had made its mark.

About that time the Chinese were beginning to make use of an article which, later, in the seventeenth century, came under the generic term of Flag, Flagg, Flagge, or Vlag, depending whether you were Norseman, Swede, German or Dutch.

They used it in the Orient on land to marshal armies, and also to conduct operations, as the Greek admiral had done with his cloak.

Gradually the flag spread to Europe. First it embellished the Roman military standards where it hung from a transverse bar at the head of the staff, decorated with silver charms and battle honours, and even portraits of the reigning emperors. The pride and significance of Regimental Colours seems to emanate from such occasions as when in 103 B.C. Caius Marius assigned the Eagle exclusively to the Roman legions.

Sometimes the design was too vivid, revealing too readily the identification of those who bore the standards. In a naval action off Marseilles, in 49 B.C., Brutus was commanding Caesar's fleet against the Massilians who represented Pompey. Brutus' flagship was immediately recognised by his flamboyant standards, and she narrowly escaped being rammed by two triremes simultaneously.

With the growth of Christianity, these standards became sacred. They resided in Temples and Churches. When Colours were presented to a regiment, prayers were offered and a solemn service was held. After battle the colours were returned tattered and scarred to their churches. The custom still survives. In St. Giles Cathedral, Edinburgh, today several score of Colours rest, never to be removed until there is nothing left but the staff on which they are borne.

The eleventh century produced other Standards which, though connected with Christianity, could certainly never have entered a church. These were the great cumbersome structures which appeared in the Crusades. One which bore the Personal Flag of Richard I, in a battle near Acre in 1191 consisted of "a very large beam like the mast of a ship, placed upon four wheels in a frame very solidly fastened together and bound with iron, so that it seems incapable of yielding either to sword, axe, or fire."

As long as everyone saw the banner borne aloft they knew their leader was safe and all was well. The structure was defended by a specially selected bodyguard. In battle it was also a refuge. "Hither the sick were brought and cured, hither were brought the wounded, and even famous or illustrious men tired out in the fighting."

Colours are frequently mentioned in connection with banners and standards. Gold, purple, and red are the most prominent. Early evidence of red being used as a definite signal comes from the voyages of the Cabots. In A.D. 1020 when Karlsefni, Bjarni and Thorbjorn sailed to the westward from Iceland they were probably just as surprised to strike the American coast as the inhabitants were to see them. When the Vikings approached, so long as they displayed white shields all was peace, but the moment red shields were shown it was taken by the Indians as a general signal for battle.

To the Crusaders, red seemed to have a more gruesome significance. Apart from the mobile standards, personal banners were carried into battle by kings and noblemen. These banners, which were usually white, were attached to sword or spear. The speed at which they changed from white to red gave some indication of how their owners were faring.

So far these historical examples have been more military than naval. At this stage we go afloat. Let us embark with William Duke of Normandy on board *Mora* at St. Valery, in the estuary of the Somme, late on the afternoon of 27th September, 1066.

As he did not wish to reach the English coast before daybreak, the Duke ordered his ships to anchor round him on making the open sea. At the appointed time the signal to proceed with the invasion of England was made by lighting a lantern at *Mora's* masthead followed by the sounding of a trumpet. This seems worthier of such an occasion than what happened when the next successful invasion across the channel was launched 878 years later, by a nod from a meteorologist.

That important historical monument, the Bayeux Tapestry, which has survived since A.D. 1150, shows William Duke of Normandy's ship after he was promoted to Conqueror. She is distinguished by a blue-bordered white banner with a golden cross. Other ships are shown flying the personal flags of the knights who accompanied him. This gay flourish seems a fitting introduction to the Royal Navy.

The first authority on the subject of signalling in our Navy is the *Black Book of the Admiralty*, which appeared in A.D. 1338, and is still in existence. Before looking at it we must remember that, in those days, this country was a long way behind our contemporaries in the Mediterranean, who were backed by Greek and Roman tradition and encouraged by Mediterranean weather.

Take, for example, the intelligent grasp which Emperor Leo VI had three hundred years previously on the matter of signalling at sea. "Let there be some standard in your ship," he insisted, "either a banner or a streamer or something else in some conspicuous position, to the end you may be able thereby to make known what requires to be done." He then suggests appropriate signals for what does require to be done to control a fleet at sea. He finishes, "And thus, O general, let the exercise of these signals be practised, so that all officers in command of ships under you may have certain knowledge of all such signs, . . . so that well familiarised with the signals, they may readily understand them in time of emergency and carry out the orders indicated."

At least these instructions laid the foundations for reasonable communication between ships, whereas three hundred years later our *Black Book* contained only two single flag signals.

(1) "Also it is to be noted that at whatever convenient time it pleases the admiral to call together the captains and masters of the fleet to take counsel with them he will carry high in the middle of the mast of his ship a banner of council so that in all parts of the fleet, whether in port or out at sea, this may be recognised and perceived, etc., and then immediately the captains and masters of ships are bound to assemble without delay with their boats well manned with seamen to row and go on board the ship of the admiral there to hear and do what the council of the admiral shall have ordained."

(2) "In case any ship or other vessel of the fleet perceive any enemy vessel upon the sea then he shall put a banner aloft by which the ship of the admiral and other ships of the fleet may have knowledge that he has seen one or more enemy vessels and thus afterwards give the best orders they know to encounter it."

This comparison shows that while in the Mediterranean tactics and manœuvre were understood, and signals existed to implement them, nothing so subtle had occurred to us. Our ships were tougher and less manœuvrable. If trouble cropped up they closed one another and conferred with their admiral to decide what to do.

In 1420 Mocenigo, Captain General of the Venetian Navy, imposed a fine of ten lire on ships in formation passing their next ahead without orders. In 1575 Antoine de Conflans reported strange ships in more detail by showing as many banners as the number of sails sighted on the side they had been seen. At home the positioning of sails conveyed a particular meaning, and the cannon was used to attract attention. "If by chance the said ships have parted company, which God forbid, and meet again by day, the one to windward shall lower and raise the topsail once and fire one gun. The one to leeward shall lower and raise the said topsail once and fire two guns."

Some of our naval traditions spring from instructions issued at this time. "If the said Lord and his fleet encounter enemy fleets where they must fight, they shall show all the ensigns and banners they have, so that each one may do his duty"; and again, "Let no vessel salute another while it is in sight of the said Lord, on pain of corporal punishment."

In 1530 "Orders to be used in the King's Majestie's Navy by the sea" added, "When and at all tymes the admyrall will anker or disanker, he must shote a pece, that thereby the rest may know to do the same; and that no shippe ride in anothers walke, for in that is greate danger."

". . . If it chance any shippe in the night fall in leake, or breake his maste, he may shote a pece of Ordinance or two to warne the flete he hath harme and in perall, to the extent he may have help, and the rest to tarie."

". . . If in the night there chanceth any enemyes unlooked for to fall into the flete, he that first doth askrie the same shall shote off two peces, and give a token of two fires and by that token shall he understande that they be enemyes that be in the flete. If they do flee, let everie man make after, and that shippe that is nighest beare a light in his stearnye that the rest may know whither the enemye goeth, for otherwise they may lose them; and if he that giveth the chace, see not the fleete follow, let him shote a pece, that they may follow by his shotte, in case they should not see his light."

By this time we had caught up on our Mediterranean contemporaries. Signalling at sea in our Navy had, in fact, advanced about as far as our unwieldy ships allowed. It was up to the constructors and the seamen to make the next move. Ships had reached the same relative stage of development as tanks in the 1914-18 war. They were not used tactically and collectively; they were independent units which fought their own way through. In fact, in July, 1588, when the Spanish Armada was off Plymouth, tactical instructions did not exist in our Navy.

It was not until the 1650's that naval tactics began to take shape, and more signals became necessary. Orders for the line ahead formation were issued over the signatures of Blake, Deane and Monck. In 1653 Admiral Blake used the five most prominent parts of his ship to hoist about twenty-five different manœuvring signals. Throughout the rest of that century flags of different colours and designs appeared. James, Duke of York, later James II, took a great interest. In 1673 he co-ordinated all the existing signal flags, which by that time were far too numerous to remember, and he issued the first signal book, a copy of which exists today in the Admiralty library. In 1714 Jonathan Greenwood went one better. He edited a pocket signal book in which, he boasted, he had "disposed matters in such a manner that any instruction may be found in half a minute."

Throughout the eighteenth century the Navy developed rapidly. The increasing flexibility and requirements of the fleet could no longer be dealt with by a few flags in strongly contrasted designs appearing in prominent positions. More signals were needed but there was no room to hoist them. In 1746 there were sixteen flags is use to express 144 signals. In 1780 there were fifty flags expressing about 330.

In 1776 a complete revolution in signalling methods was

inaugurated by Admiral Lord Howe. He issued a signal book in which the total number of flags was twenty-one. Many of these were of new design. In this book he grouped and numbered each instruction and numbered each page so that any instruction could be signalled by quoting its number and the page on which it appeared. The idea was opposed by some Flag Officers who thought that several flags on one hoist could not be read at any distance. They maintained the scheme did not compare with the simplicity of single flags in prominent positions. Nevertheless Lord Howe's ideas began to take hold. Improvements and variations in flag design were also introduced by Kempenfelt and Sir Charles Knowles. Great personal interest was taken in the subject. It soon became customary for Flag Officers to draw up and print their own instructions when they took over a command. Each particular operation received a suitable set of signals to go with it. "While you remain in this service you will establish such signals and instructions for the government of the ships under your command as you may think fit," said Howe when he gave Kempenfelt his orders for the command of a detached Squadron on 30th April, 1782.

Howe's interest continued and he revised his ideas periodically. His latest signal code was in use in the fleet under his command on the Glorious First of June, 1794. With amendments, this edition existed up to the Battles of St. Vincent and the Nile.

Perhaps the best testimony to Howe's efforts is given in a letter from Nelson in reply to Howe's congratulations on the victory of the Nile. "By attacking the enemy's van and centre, the wind blowing directly along their line, I was enabled to throw what force I pleased on a few ships. This plan my friends conceived by the signals (for which we are principally if not entirely indebted to your Lordship) and we kept a superior force to the enemy."

In 1795, a completely new form of signalling called semaphore, devised by the Rev. Lord George Murray, was introduced into the Navy. To start with it consisted of a screen with six shutters which could be operated to give numerous combinations, and it was used ashore by the Admiralty to communicate with Portsmouth and with the Nore. The semaphore signals were relayed by a chain of signal stations in sight of one another on neighbouring hills.

In 1799 the Board of Admiralty, who hitherto had been content to allow flag officers to make their own private codes, issued the first printed signal book. It was a development of Howe's principles, with some additions from Kempenfelt and others. Its greatest asset was that it was universal, so that a ship joining a fleet need no longer fear that the signals meant nothing until a copy of that particular admiral's private code had been received on board.

By now the offensive spirit and personal skill of officers and men were being welded into squadrons which could manœuvre, concentrate, and harass with increasing efficiency. They were certainly getting plenty of practice, and each battle brought a lesson; a new manœuvre, a suggested formation. Each innovation had to be translated into instructions which could be signalled and, once again, our signal system began to feel the strain. An Admiral found he could handle a fleet in a crude fashion but he could not make his intentions clear. The language of signalling was too rigid. Captains were on their own now. Conferences at sea, or closing to trumpet range, were no longer fashionable. Steps had to be taken to make the signal language more civilised, to increase its scope of expression from the language of a child to that of an adult. These steps were taken by Sir Home Popham.

His first vocabulary contained 1,000 useful words. These were signalled by using numbers in 3- or 4-flag hoists. For the next twelve years he worked away, printing and circulating his books privately. His telegraphic signals were in use at Trafalgar.

In 1812 Sir Home Popham produced his second, and very much enlarged edition of telegraphic signals. By introducing alphabetical letters as well as numbers he increased the permutations in 3- and 4-flag hoists to a vocabulary of some 30,000 words.

These included geographical and technical tables, tables of stores and provisions. The only indication that Sir Home had a sense of humour comes from the two examples he chose for "Private Communications."

(1) BOE   YOUR
    AC8   SISTER
    852   MARRIED
    85F   TO
    C87   A LORD OF THE ADMIRALTY
(2) FAI   HAVE YOU AN IDEA?
    G647 A CHANGE OF MINISTERS IS ABOUT TO TAKE PLACE

These telegraphic signals went through ten editions before their author's death in 1848. Popham also improved the semaphore of 1795. In 1816 he introduced an instrument with arms working on two separate uprights. At night it was lit by lanterns, and messages from the Admiralty relayed through ten stations could be passed, we are told, in ten minutes.

In 1817, Captain Frederick Marryat showed that as well as being a distinguished and courageous naval officer, he had interests in signalling. He introduced the first code of signals for the Merchant Service, designing his own numeral, and later alphabetical, flags. In spite of the many revisions between his day and ours, thirteen of his flags are still in use.

The next milestone was planted in 1844. In that year the first signal to travel beyond visibility distance made a successful journey of some thirty miles on a wire stretched between Baltimore and Washington. It was propelled by electricity in a code invented by Samuel Morse. Twenty years later the Morse code was introduced into the Navy. This "make-and-break" principle was adapted to artificial light, in 1867 when Captain Colomb's flashing signal lantern appeared.

Thus, a stage had been reached afloat where intercommunication by day and night was practicable within the limits of visibility. But a unit at sea at the end of the nineteenth century was just as isolated from the world as it had been when sailing ships were invented.

Then, out of the air, came wireless.

On 1st September, 1895, Admiral Jackson, who saw great possibilities in wireless telegraphy, met Signor Marconi, who was producing practical results from experiments in that direction. On 7th May, 1898, in Admiral Jackson's presence, the sceptics were severely shaken when Marconi tied an insulated wire to a flagstaff at Bournemouth into which he pumped morse messages which were received at Alum Bay, Isle of Wight, fourteen miles away.

This achievement must have been a setback to those interested in another line of research at this time. The *Handbook of Homing Pigeons for Naval Purposes*, published the same year, began confidently by saying: "Now that the conveyance of messages by homing pigeons for naval and military purposes has become an essential part of war preparation in all European countries . . ."

Another handbook also appeared called *Working Wireless Telegraphic Apparatus*. It did not sound so confident. It explained that when receiving signals various things could happen. The signals might be satisfactory, but this was most improbable. Later on it added, to avoid confusion: "If in doubt about a signal always ask for a repetition of the doubtful words or signs. The very worst thing to do is to keep the sender waiting in suspense, for after waiting for about two minutes for your RD (message read) he will probably make another signal to you, 'Have you got last signal?' And you will probably not yet get this one either, and ask him to repeat, when he will repeat the wrong one, and so on, causing great delay."

But radio had come to stay and everyone in command of H.M. ships was soon clamouring to have it installed. In a certain cruiser the captain in his bath was made to complete the circuit physically when dockyard workmen were looking for a suitable "earth." But nothing mattered so long as the equipment was installed before the ship sailed on manœuvres. Fabulous achievements followed one after the other. The Flagship of the West Indian Squadron, eighty miles from Bermuda received R—CKSA—D shortly after Rocksand had won the Derby. By 1904 Gibraltar was reading messages from the Admiralty. Out of sight at sea was never again to be out of mind.

But there was a snag to this new magic. Visual signals and cables were reasonably secure, but a wireless message in plain language could be read by anyone who had the equipment to receive it.

This problem of security called for more codes, and with the codes came those mathematical magicians called cryptographers. They translated the language into numbers and put a new cypher into circulation whenever the existing one was in danger of becoming manageable. They have been doing this ever since. When not engaged in building up our cyphers they break down other people's with surprising skill. The intercepted signals made by the Germans at the Battle of Jutland were being decoded by Admiralty almost as rapidly as our own.

The increased security also tightened up the custody of signal books which had to be mustered, signed for, and locked up. They were fitted with lead covers so that they would sink when thrown overboard. At least they *should* sink. It alarmed a captain serving on a foreign station to find that his secret literature sank in fresh water but floated in the prevailing brine.

In the meantime the efficiency of flag signalling, semaphore and flashing, sensing the threat of the electronic monster, rose to its peak. The precision and skill of signalmen rivalled that of the gun crews; they certainly had just as much drill. It was normal to see a Flagship at sea with four pairs of mechanical semaphore arms waving, a few signal lamps flashing and streams of bunting appearing and vanishing from halyards. It looked indeed as though Admirals never stopped talking.

Today visual signalling and W/T have been joined by radio telephone, and it is obvious that the latter will kill the former. No one is going to translate messages in and out of some complicated ritual when they can be spoken conversationally, leaving the security in the hands of the mechanics.

This is the electronic age—wherever it is leading us. It has already increased the size of our forefathers' world from the horizon to something bigger than the earth. It has also enabled grunts and gestures to be transmitted, exactly as they are made, to ocean bed, stratosphere, or the ends of the earth. The original forefather who was told to look into the matter, and those who have followed him, have certainly done a good job.

II

Special Flags and Customs

Having traced the general development of signalling let us turn to its obstinacies—those means of conveying information which have resisted development; flags which originated long ago and are still with us. Some national flags, for example, can be traced back through centuries, while countries such as Germany have changed theirs twice within living memory. Leaving national flags more or less in a class by themselves, let us choose three others which have acquired a character of their own. The Royal Standard, the Banner of the Federation of the Cinque Ports, and the Jolly Roger. The first has kept its dignity through many changes for over 700 years. The second, which had great significance when it floated from the bridgehead between this country and the Continent, is now little more than a monument. The third, an international, with its sinister, brilliant design, is forever planted in fiction and occasionally reappears in fact.

THE ROYAL STANDARD

A herald is a forerunner, one who bears tidings.

A flag is a good background for the display of heraldry, it gives the herald a chance to reveal interesting facts about the character who owns the flag. It becomes a signal illustrated with recognisable symbols. The frequent appearance of the symbolic lion and the absence of the louse shows that heraldry, generally speaking, builds up its subjects.

Highest in dignity among all our flags is the one signalling the presence of the Monarch which used to be flown at sea by the Lord High Admiral.

The Royal Arms first appeared on a flag in 1189 in the form of a golden lion, the first Great Seal of King Richard I. This seal was lost during Richard's captivity, and replaced by three lions one above the other. Those heraldic beasts have appeared on every Royal Standard ever since.

They have had many associates, for the Royal Standard is a personal banner combining the federation of the realm with the ancestry of each succeeding ruler. In 1340, when Edward III acquired the throne of France, the British lions were joined—and for a while dominated—by the Fleurs de Lys. On Edward III's death the design shrank to make way for the Cross of Edward the Confessor. Perhaps Henry IV found that he could not live up to such piety, for, in his reign, the Cross disappeared.

Then came the Stuarts, with the Scottish lion extremely rampant at being placed in the second quarter. The Irish harp, which first appeared at the funeral of Queen Elizabeth, was added to represent a Kingdom which, in historical fact, had never been under one King.

After a period of Cromwellian austerity, William III added his own private lion of Nassau to the Stuart banner, raising the Pride of heraldic lions to fourteen on one Standard. Queen Anne reverted to the Stuart design and, after the union with Scotland, the Scottish lion was more amiably housed in the same quarter as his English contemporaries.

On the accession of George I one of these quarters had to give place to the arms of Hanover, which introduced three more lions and a white horse. In 1801 this Standard was revised, and the three British lions bade farewell to the golden lilies of France after an association of 461 years, some of which had been spent in armed conflict between the two countries.

Queen Victoria removed the Hanoverian embellishment, and so the Royal Standard remains today, with the three British lions still "passant guardant in pale" in quarters 1 and 4, the Scottish lion still rampant in the second quarter, and the harp, which was never an authentic symbol of Ireland, in the third quarter.

The reason given by a special commission in 1911 as to why Wales is not represented was that Wales is a Principality and not a Kingdom. In that case the harp's position does not look very secure.

Will those restless British lions ever settle down for good?

THE BANNER OF THE CINQUE PORTS

After invading England, the Normans showed their intention of closing the back door, and guarding the south-east corner of Britain by fortifying the towns of Hastings, Sandwich, Dover, Romney and Hythe.

As far back as Edward the Confessor a charter was issued, and granted by successive sovereigns, calling upon the Barons of these towns to maintain the fortifications, and to provide "their full service of 57 ships at their own cost for 15 days, when summoned by Ourself or Our Heirs." In return they received certain enviable privileges which set them free from the general legal system of the realm, and granted them a handsome cut on the price of wine.

This banded the Cinque Ports together under one banner, and they have remained so ever since. Chief of the Barons was the Lord Warden who also became Admiral of the Cinque Ports fleet. Today the flag of the Cinque Ports only flies from Walmer Castle, and never at sea. Since 1941 Sir Winston Churchill, K.G., has been the Lord Warden.

In the original banner the three British lions suffered severe heraldic treatment. The banner shows them emerging into a scarlet void from a blue one. In crossing over, the poor creatures

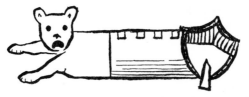

have been dimidiated and their sterns have become the sterns of ships. Today, the lions are there, still looking rather surprised. Four castles, a ship, a crown and an anchor have been added.

THE JOLLY ROGER

Thieving in the open started as soon as people began carrying valuables about. Piracy started when they took their valuables to sea. No ocean has been free from pirates. They have appeared, thrived, and been suppressed on every seaboard. Years ago Piracy passed as maritime adventure. The Phœnicians combined piracy with enterprise. In Homeric days it was a reputable, even a dignified calling. Gradually it came to be frowned upon. From the eighth to the eleventh centuries the Norsemen became the terror of our western coast. In the Mediterranean, Algiers became a pirate stronghold. The racket spread. The Corsairs struck out towards our shores. Lundy Island became a pirate's nest. On they came, up the Channel to Ireland, to Iceland and across the Atlantic. For three centuries they infested the High Seas.

The exact moment when pirates were banded together under one distinguishing flag is obscure. So is the date that the Skull and Cross-bones on a Black ground were accepted as the design for this flag. As far as heraldry is concerned, however, one must congratulate the designer. It seems to convey the whole calling in a flash. It seems appropriate to fly over gentlemen like Captain

Teach, with "that large quantity of hair like a frightful Meteor," covering his face, which "frightened America more than any Comet." It seems to blend with Captain Edward Low's treatment of the master of a whale-boat whom he captured off Rhode Island —he cut off his ears and made him eat them with pepper and salt— "which hard injunction he complied with without making a word."

The early part of the eighteenth century was a colourful time in the history of pirates. In the West Indies especially there was plenty of shipping and valuable cargoes. Merchantmen in that area had a grim gauntlet to run.

The Pirate technique was to fly some national colours and approach a merchant ship. At the appropriate moment the bogus colours would be struck and replaced by the Black flag—and the merchant ship's number was generally up.

Occasionally the pirates did not have it their own way; sometimes they got a shock. Pirate Captain Charles Vane "fell upon a ship, which 'twas expected would have struck as soon as our black colours were hoisted; but instead of that she discharged a Broadside, and hoisted Colours, which shewed her to be a French Man of War." Vane desired to have nothing further to say to her, but trimm'd his sails and stood away from the Frenchman; "but Monsieur, having a mind to be better informed who he was, set all his sails and crowded after him. During the chase the Pyrates were divided in their resolutions what to do, Vane the Captain, was for making off as fast as he could, alledging the Man of War was too strong to cope with . . . so the Brigantine having the heels, as they term it, of the French man, she came clear off."

Periodically there was a big clean up. On Monday, 5th February, 1721, H.M.S. *Swallow* found the pirate ships *Ranger* and *Royal Sovereign*. Having forced them to submit she took some 300 prisoners, who later stood their trial, and 52 were executed.

But, on the whole, the Black Flag Industry at that time flourished, and the design upon the flag varied with the different pirate leaders. They each had their own house flag. The rascal

Captain Bartho Roberts, for example, had a flag "with his own figure portrayed standing upon two skulls and under them the letters ABH and AMH, signifying A BARBADIAN'S HEAD and A MARTINICAN'S HEAD." The flag which the *Swallow* captured had —"the figure of a Skeleton on it, and a man portrayed with a flaming sword in his hand, intimating a Defiance on Death itself." On promotion, Pirate Captain Spriggs had "a black Ensign made which they called Jolly Roger, with a white Skeleton in the middle of it, with a dart in one hand striking a bleeding heart, and in the other an Hour-glass." The hour glass was a symbol of the time allowed for victims to choose between joining the pirates or taking the consequences. Chains and Battle-axes appeared on other flags. The nearest approach to the design we know today belonged to Pirate Chief Worley, who had "a black Ensign with a white Death's Head in the middle of it," but no cross bones. When those thigh bones were added is not clear.

Neither is it clear why this awe-inspiring flag should have such a cheerful name; though the derivation of Jolly Roger is probably not so gay as it sounds. Jolly could be taken as meaning "to flatter with intention of deceiving"; Roger could be connected with the word Rogue.

In both World Wars the Jolly Roger has reappeared. With great personal pride, and with official tolerance if not blessing, it has flown from our submarines returning from their patrols. A submarine in war time, like the pirate, is nobody's friend. By adding symbols to represent the ships they had sunk, submariners found an appropriate way to express their defiance.

SIGNAL FLAGS

There are other flags which appear singly or in groups, past or present, which have acquired character.

SPECIAL FLAGS AND CUSTOMS

The versatile Church Pennant, for example. It is easily distinguishable and depending on when and where it appears it proclaims that either the ship's company is at divine service, the ship is letting go or weighing anchor, or that someone has fallen overboard. Colours have their own significance. A Red flag is symbolic of mutiny. It has been used twice by the Royal Navy; once at Portsmouth, and once at the Nore in 1797. It is interesting to note that it was struck on 4th June in honour of the King's birthday, and rehoisted the following day. A white flag means amity and goodwill; a truce amid strife; surrender when the cause is lost. A yellow flag denotes infection or quarantine.

Pairs of flags can have single meanings. The flags change, but the impressive meanings remain—"Raise steam with all despatch." "Proceed in execution of previous orders." "Pay particular attention to the Admiral, who may alter course or speed without signal." At one time NJ meant "Manœuvre well executed." With a negative flag above it it meant the opposite. In either case as soon as it appeared at the flagship's halyards it was repeated by all ships present together with the pennants of the ship to which it referred. The whole world knew whether that ship had done well or badly. Another signal with remarkable penetration is "Indicate the name of Officer of the Watch." This is the recognised reproof for a ship behaving erratically or getting out of station. It must have brought many Captains up on many bridges in great haste and in great heat.

Private signals with private meanings are not permitted as in Lord Howe's day, yet they appear occasionally to meet special circumstances. Between the wars a certain destroyer had the frequent task of steaming through a practice area in which submarines attacked her with dummy torpedoes. After each attack the submarine surfaced in the destroyer's wake anxious for a quick assessment of her attack. To give this assessment without wasting time the destroyer hoisted a large raspberry fashioned in basket work. If it appeared the right way up it meant the attack was a failure. The position in which it appeared indicated how it

31

had failed. An inverted raspberry at the masthead meant a successful attack.

General Drill has a signal routine of its own. These drills are tasks, initiated by signal, carried out competitively between ships in a squadron or flotilla. The tasks naturally have to suit the ships taking part, and on this occasion private signals are allowed. In the signal book there is a general drill table, where suitable tasks are entered against the flags which initiate them. The tasks, which demand prodigious feats of seamanship from large bodies of men, are carried out at full speed and full pressure. The ships and their crews are tied in knots.

The general drill signal table can be designed to cater for all tastes. Here are some examples:

CHIEF COOK TO REPORT ON BOARD FLAGSHIP WITH FRIED EGG.

CHAPLAINS PADDLE ROUND THEIR SHIPS ON CARLEY RAFTS.

SECURE CAPTAIN IN STRAIT JACKET AND SEND HIM TO FLAGSHIP.

LAND ALL HEADS OF DEPARTMENTS. NEXT SENIOR TAKE OVER.

SPECIAL CUSTOMS

Many customs have grown up round our national colours.

Saluting them at sea, for example, has had an historic background.

In 1201 King John decreed that if his Admiral should meet any ship at sea which refused to lower their sails at command, their crews should be reputed as enemies and their ships and cargoes should be forfeited.

Many decrees and incidents followed before this practical method of demanding submission changed into a signal of respect. Eventually the seafaring community of all nations submitted ungrudgingly to the Royal Navy by dipping their colours whenever they met on the high seas. But the Navy earned that respect the hard way.

In 1554, for example, a Spanish Fleet of 160 sail was escorting their King Philip on his way to England to marry Queen Mary, when he was met by an English Fleet commanded by Lord William Howard, Lord High Admiral. When the Spaniards passed without paying the customary honours, Lord Howard signalled his twenty-eight ships to prepare for action, and fired a round shot into the hull of the Spanish Flagship. The Spaniards immediately saluted.

In 1652 Admiral Blake met a Dutch Squadron under Admiral Van Tromp in the Channel. As the latter did not salute, Blake fired two shots across his bow. A third followed which Van Tromp declared struck his ship and wounded a man. Battle ensued and the first Dutch war was launched. When it was over the Dutch agreed to strike their flags and lower their topsails on meeting our ships in the British seas.

Our stubborn demands rankled with the French. Louis XIV did his best to induce Charles II to dispense with this compulsory salute to British men-o'-war. Charles II seemed surprised at the idea. Writing to his sister, the Duchess of Orleans, at the French Court, he says, "I extremely wonder at that you writ to me, for certainly never any ship refused to strike when they met any ships belonging to the Crown of England. That is right well known, and never disputed by any King before."

In the eighteenth century, the decree still ran—"when any of His Majesty's ships shall meet with any ship or ships belonging to any foreign Prince within His Majesty's seas (which extend to Cape Finisterre) it is expected that the said foreign ships do strike their topsail and take in their flag, in acknowledgment of His Majesty's Sovereignty in those seas; and if any shall refuse or offer to resist it is enjoined to all Flag Officers and Commanders to use their utmost endeavours to compel them thereto, and not suffer any dishonour to be done to His Majesty." The Merchant-men also had to toe the line—"And if any of His Majesty's subjects shall so much forget their duty as to omit striking their topsail in passing by His Majesty's ships, the name of the ship and master, and from whence and whither bound, together with affidavits of the fact, are to be sent up to the Secretary of the Admiralty, in order to proceed against them in the Admiralty court." After Trafalgar, British Naval Power stood at such a height that no loss of prestige could possibly arise from easing these regulations, so the salute was no longer demanded. Today Merchant ships dip their Colours to warships and to each other as an act of courtesy.

Half-masting of Colours does not seem to have gone back as far as saluting. After the Restoration it was a custom in the Navy to observe the anniversary of the execution of Charles I by lowering Colours to "halfe staff high"; but in 1586 the *Black Pinnace* which brought the body of Sir Philip Sidney from Holland is shown with a black flag at the main top masthead.

Striking Colours as a signal of submission seems also to be comparatively modern. In the olden days, before the gun, when fighting was hand-to-hand at close quarters, the battle raged till one side gave in. Everyone was much too busy to notice whether their Colours were flying or not. It was not until sea battles were fought by gun at a distance that a ship hauled down her colours to show that her internal state was beyond hope and that further loss of life seemed pointless.

During the French wars it was customary to hoist our own Colours above those of a captured enemy, either at the peak or ensign staff.

More recently, a German trawler was captured off the Danish coast by a destroyer in 1915 and was steaming into an East Coast harbour with a prize crew. The custom had obviously been forgotten by the local fishermen for they fired on the German Ensign, although the White Ensign flew above it.

Captured Colours at sea, as on land, are treated with reverence. The flags of many Spanish Galleons were paraded at a

Thanksgiving Service attended by Queen Elizabeth after the defeat of the Armada.

In the seventeenth century it was considered a proper thing to decorate a ship with the flags of captured enemies. A certain Captain Heaton supported this custom. He was in command of H.M.S. *Sapphire* . . . "in which ship he took so many prizes that on a festival day the yards, stays, backstays, and shrouds being hung with Dutch, French, Spanish and Burgundian Colours and pennants variously intermixed, and the English Colours and pennants spread, made a beautiful show and raised the courage of all belonged to her."

Successful racing yacht owners of today still follow in the footsteps of Captain Heaton.

Naval History by Signal

AN OUTSIDE OPINION
1779

This incident is related by a civilian who sailed on a cruise in the flagship of the Channel Fleet.

Benjamin Thompson, scientist, who afterwards became Count Von Rumford, came to England from Boston in 1776. He was interested in Ballistics, and his friend, Lord George Germain, Secretary of State for the Colonies, thought he might help with the development of naval gunnery. Accordingly, a cruise was arranged for him in H.M.S. *Victory* as the personal guest of Admiral Sir Charles Hardy, who commanded the Channel Fleet.

On 20th July, 1779, while at sea, he wrote to Lord George as follows:

"My dear Lord,—I can stand it no longer. Those who are interested in the disgrace of our Commander may laugh at our blunders, but I, who do not feel those prejudices which are but too common in the profession, am hurt beyond measure to find how little dependance is to be put in our skill in manoeuvring this great and respectable Fleet. I have this morning been put out of all manner of patience. You must know we never as yet had attempted but one single manoeuvre and that is to draw the ships into line of battle, one directly ahead of the other, and upon a signal to tack about all together. In this we never have succeeded. It has always been more than two hours before the ships ahead have got into their stations, the line has always been very crooked and the ships at very unequal distances and when we have come to put about confusion has commonly ensued, and we have been obliged to end our manœuvring abruptly by making the signal for the ships to return to their stations in the order of sailing. This has arisen sometimes from one cause, and sometimes from another but I don't remember a single instance in which we have attempted to manœuvre when we did not make at least one evidently wrong and contradictory signal. I thought we might possibly succeed better in divisions, and accordingly this morning after breakfast I contrived to hint this idea in the gentlest manner possible to the Admiral, Captain Kempenfelt being present. I received no answer, but about half an hour after the Captain came down and proposed the measure to the Admiral. It was very well, but how to give the necessary orders was the difficulty. The signals for the three divisions could not be made together—if the centre division was formed first that signal might then be hauled down and the signal for the Vice Admiral's Division to form might be made, and afterwards that of the Rear in the same manner. I saw in this way of proceeding the day would be much too short for the manœuvre. Captain Kempenfelt was silent. The Admiral looked at him for some time without saying a word. I saw no kind of difficulty in the thing. The printed book of signals lay upon the table. I took it up, and turning over the leaves pointed with my finger to the following passage:—

'If at any time I would point out that the signals made, relate to a particular division of the fleet, I will signify the same as follows—

'If to the division of the Admiral commanding in chief.'	*A Dutch flag with a red flag under it*
'If to the division of the Flag commanding in the second Post.'	*A Dutch flag with a white flag under it*
'If to the division of the Flag post.'	*A Dutch flag with a blue flag under it.*

and why not, (said I modestly) make the signal for the line of battle, and at the same time hoist the three signals for the three divisions in different parts of the ship? They made me no answer. Capt. Kempenfelt went upon deck. The Admiral took his hat and followed him. I was neither surprised nor angry that my proposal was not taken notice of. Why should I expect that my advice should be taken when nobody's else in the ship, or in the fleet is either asked, or suffered? In a few minutes I heard a gun, and going upon deck, saw a flag half blue, half white flying at the mizen peak, and a Dutch flag with a red flag under it at the mizen-top-mast head. This signal was soon repeated by all the flagships in the Fleet and their repeating frigates (as are all signals made by the Commander in Chief). The *Royal George* was just upon our weather quarter. As she is always to lead our division in a line of battle ahead upon the starboard tack, it was expected she would make more sail in order to go ahead into her station. Instead of this she laid her sails aback and was preparing to hoist out a boat. The Admiral had the fidgets to a most violent degree. Captain Kempenfelt, in a great passion, called out to the lieutenant who had the watch to hail the *Peggy* cutter, and order her to go alongside the *Royal George* and desire Sir John Ross to make sail and go ahead into his station. The Admiral, not willing to hurt Sir John's feelings too much by a public reprimand, or perhaps from some other motive, altered the order by giving directions for the master of the cutter to go aboard the *Royal George* and tell Sir John Ross that he was out of his station. Happily the *Peggy* was not within hail and the signal was obliged to be made to bring her to the *Victory*. This took up time and before she could come up with us we found out that instead of a signal for a line of battle ahead we had made a signal for the weekly returns of the ships of the Admiral's division. The Admiral was in Capt. Kempenfelt's cabin when the discovery was made or rather when the laugh became general upon the quarter-deck. At that moment I would have given all I was worth in the world to have been at Stoneland, or anywhere else but on board the *Victory*. To paint my feelings would be totally impossible. To see those one is living with upon the most friendly footing a subject of derision to the whole world is really very painful. I was happy however that the *Peggy* had not received her orders, and the first thing to be done was to inform the Admiral of the mistake. This nobody would undertake. There was no time to be lost and I determined to do it myself. I accordingly plucked up courage and went into Capt. Kempenfelt's cabin, but I found the Admiral and the Captain so busy looking over the signal book together that I did not dare interrupt them. I went again upon the deck and prevailed upon Captain Collins to do the business. The best thing to have done would have been to have stood by the signal as it was and received the weekly returns. . . . Though there was not an officer in the fleet who did not see the blunder we made, yet there was not a ship of our division which did not send in her weekly account. It was curious to see the stifled grin of the Lieutenant as he gave these to Capt. Kempenfelt and the spiteful manner in which the latter snatched them out of his hand."

(*Naval Miscellany, III, Navy Records Society, 1928.*)

THE BATTLE OF
THE GLORIOUS FIRST OF JUNE,
1794

After two weeks' cruising, the Channel Fleet, consisting of 26 ship-of-the-line under Admiral Lord Howe, looked into Brest. On 17th May, they learnt that the French Fleet had sailed to protect a large and valuable convoy from North America and the West Indies. Lord Howe immediately followed them on the course they had taken out into the Atlantic.

A few ships previously captured by the French were met and recaptured. From these and other sources, the Admiral estimated

THREE DECK LINE-OF-BATTLE SHIP · 100 GUNS

THE BATTLE OF
THE GLORIOUS FIRST OF JUNE 1794

SHIPS TAKING PART

QUEEN CHARLOTTE (*flagship*) · 100
ROYAL SOVEREIGN · 100
ROYAL GEORGE · 100
BARFLEUR · 98
IMPREGNABLE · 98
QUEEN · 98
GLORY · 98

GIBRALTAR · 80
CAESAR · 80
BELLEREPHON · 74
MONTAGU · 74
TREMENDOUS · 74
VALIANT · 74
RAMILLIES · 74
AUDACIOUS · 74
BRUNSWICK · 74
ALFRED · 74
DEFENCE · 74
LEVIATHAN · 74
MAJESTIC · 74
INVINCIBLE · 74
ORION · 74
RUSSELL · 74
MARLBOROUGH · 74
THUNDERER · 74
CULLODEN · 74

TWO DECK LINE-OF-BATTLE SHIP · 74 GUNS

PHAETON · 38
LATONA · 38
NIGER · 32
SOUTHAMPTON · 32
VENUS · 32
AQUILLON · 32
PEGASUS · 32

FRIGATE · 32 GUNS

the position of the French Fleet. Fading hopes were revived when the enemy was sighted soon after daylight on Wednesday, 28th May.

Signalling in the Royal Navy had just been revolutionised by Howe himself, and the latest edition of his code was in use at

------

Narrative

Wednesday 28th May

A.M. At dawn *Bellerophon* (74 guns), Flagship of the detached fast sailing squadron, sent the frigates to look out.

4.00 Flagship (*Queen Charlotte*, 100 guns), logs strong wind from SSW, cloudy, course ESE. All the fleet in sight.

4.30 *Phaeton* (Frigate) shortened sail to interrogate a brig. Found her to be *Wilmington* of Campbelltown from Cadiz bound for London. Another strange sail sighted to windward.

8.0 *Queen* (98 guns) sighted strange Fleet of large ships standing towards her. At first the ships seemed to be coming down in a confused manner, as though not expecting it to be the British Fleet they had in view. It was some time before they formed into any regular line of battle.

8.39 Flagship sighted enemy fleet 12 to 15 miles to windward on Easterly course, forming line of battle.

Phaeton cleared for action, carried away her fore topsail

the time. This is the first occasion on which signals were used to control our Fleet in battle.

The following signals made and received by the flagship *Queen Charlotte* are recorded opposite a narrative of events extracted from the logs and reports of ships which took part in the action.

———————

Signals

Wednesday 28th May
A.M.

5.00 *From Latona (Frigate)*
STRANGE SAIL BEARING SE

6.30 *From Russell (74 guns)*
STRANGE SAIL BEARING SE

7.30 *From Phaeton (Frigate)*
STRANGE SAIL BEARING SSE

7.35 *From Latona*
STRANGE FLEET BEARING SSW

8.25 *To Bellerophon*
RECONNOITRE ENEMY SHIPS IN VIEW AND REPORT TO THE ADMIRAL

8.34 *General*
ENEMY IN SIGHT

yard which she threw overboard, together with a hen-coop, a bittacle, a pantry, and a bulkhead, in order to clear ship. When *Bellerophon* had shortened sail, as ordered by signal, and called in the frigates, she noted the enemy Fleet in line ahead with our fleet, three or four miles to leeward in the order of sailing under a press of sail.

10.22 *Majestic* (74 guns) observed by Flagship with three reefs in her topsails, her fore topsail yard bending like a bow.

11.14 Some of the Enemy ships observed changing stations in the line.

11.50 Flagship counted 31 sail of the Enemy.

Noon Fleet estimated to be W by S, 350 miles from Ushant.

P.M.
1.0 Fresh gales squally. Flagship split jib in a squall. A great head sea. Double reefed topsails.

1.50 Enemy altered course to Southward.

2.00 The whole Fleet in chase of the French, hoping to bring on a general action by attacking the rear with our fast-sailing ships.

3.3 *Russell* hoisted her colours and opened fire on the rear of the Enemy's line. Fire was returned. *Bellerophon* tacked before the rear enemy ship was on her beam, which brought her immediately into action.

NAVAL HISTORY BY SIGNAL

8.45 *General*
PREPARE FOR BATTLE

9.45 *To Bellerophon*
SHORTEN SAIL

9.46 *From Russell*
ESTIMATE 22 SHIPS OF THE LINE

10.28 *General*
WEATHERMOST SHIPS TO TACK FIRST REMAINDER IN SUCCES-
SION

11.13 *General*
THE PEOPLE HAVE TIME FOR THE NEXT MEAL

P.M.

1.40 *General*
ATTACK AND HARASS THE ENEMY'S REAR

1.52 *General*
CHASE

1.56 *General*
TAKE SUITABLE STATIONS FOR MUTUAL SUPPORT AND
ENGAGE THE ENEMY AS ARRIVING UP WITH THEM IN SUCCES-
SION

6.0   *Bellerophon* was still closely engaged. She had received considerable damage and had to break off to repair masts and rigging.

8.3   *Audacious* (74) engaged three-decked Frenchman (*Revolutionnaire*, 110 guns) until 9.50 when Frenchman ceased fire and struck her Colours, but *Audacious* was too disabled to take possession of her. *Thunderer*, coming to *Audacious'* assistance hailed the Frenchman and asked him if he had struck. He assured *Thunderer* in English that he had—and that he would follow during the night. No more was seen of this ship. Firing ceased on both sides at 9.0.

Nothing further was heard of the disabled Audacious either, until she reappeared in Plymouth Sound on 4th June.

British ships carried a stiff sail all night in pursuit of the French.

At midnight the enemy's lights were visible 5 miles to windward.

Thursday 29th May

Dawn. Flagship noted that *Audacious* had disappeared; wind still fresh, heavy swell.

46

4.37 *General*
EACH SHIP IS TO CARRY A LIGHT THE ENSUING NIGHT AND
REPEAT SIGNALS MADE BY THE ADMIRAL

7.19 *General*
KEEP THE ENEMY IN SIGHT. MAKE THEIR MOTIONS KNOWN
BY DAY OR NIGHT TO THE ADMIRAL

7.25 *To Russell and Marlborough (74 guns)*
ASSIST BELLEROPHON ALREADY IN ACTION

7.30 *General*
FORM LINE OF BATTLE AHEAD AND ASTERN OF THE ADMIRAL
AS MOST CONVENIENT WITHOUT REGARD TO ESTABLISHED
FORMATION

7.33 *To Marlborough, Bellerophon and Leviathan (74 guns)*
LEAVE OFF CHASE

(The last two signals were repeated at first light on
Thursday, 29th May.)

The Admiral estimated he had made sufficient advance on the Enemy to go about and menace the rear ships.

The Admiral's plan to bring about a general action in this manner began to materialise. At 7.48 the Enemy, who were now in line of battle course South, began to wear and shape a northerly course to protect their rear.

8.15 *Caesar* (80 guns, leading ship) and *Queen* (98 guns) in action with enemy's rear.

8.50 All British Fleet on port tack.

10.20 Enemy's van engaging ours at long range.

10.50 Our van returning fire.

Noon Wind S by W fresh gales. S 80° W, 300 miles from Ushant.

P.M.

1.13 Flagship observed *Caesar* did not answer the signal which was flying.

1.30 Flagship tacked and kept close to the wind to close the Enemy, and cut through their line ahead of the 5th ship. Other ships attempted to follow, but *Bellerophon* was the only other ship which succeeded. She passed between 2nd and 3rd ship. *Queen Charlotte* then tacked and chased a three-decked ship bearing an Admiral's flag, flooding her own lower deck through her lower gun ports.

Thursday 29th May
A.M.

6.57   *General*
       TACK IN SUCCESSION

7.23   *General*
       SHIPS ARE AT LIBERTY TO FIRE ON THE ENEMY THOUGH NOT
       MEANT TO BRING THEM TO GENERAL ACTION IMMEDIATELY

8.6   *To Caesar*
       MAKE MORE SAIL

8.30   *To Caesar*
       MAKE MORE SAIL

P.M.

12.16 *General*
       TACK IN SUCCESSION

1.8   *To Caesar*
       ENGAGE ENEMY'S CENTRE

1.13   *General*
       THE ADMIRAL INTENDS TO PASS THROUGH THE ENEMY'S
       LINE TO OBTAIN THE WEATHER-GAGE

2.20   *General*
       TACK IN SUCCESSION

49

3.00   By this time fog was coming down. Having outsailed the French and confused their line, the Admiral decided to break off the action and give his damaged ships a chance to patch themselves up.

5.00   Our fleet on port tack. Enemy Fleet on same tack to leeward.

Friday 30th May

Mainly thick fog all day with occasional clear patches. French Fleet was reported to be bearing NW about 9 miles distant.

Saturday 31st May

A.M.

4.00   Fog still thick; only two ships in sight. All hands busy making good defects (except, apparently for two men in *Culloden*. *Culloden's* log states—Punished Richard Alfred and Dan Malone with 18 lashes for fighting).

P.M.

4.00   Fog cleared. Enemy forming line of battle 5 or 6 miles to leeward.

2.50 *General*
     CHASE

3.00 *General*
     ACTION OVER CLOSE ADMIRAL

6.15 *General*
     LEAVE OFF CHASE

Friday 30th May
A.M.

9.10 *General*
     ENEMY IN SIGHT

9.18 *General*
     FORM LINE OF BATTLE

9.30 *General*
     SHIPS ASTERN MAKE MORE SAIL

P.M.

7.43 *General*
     CLOSE ROUND ADMIRAL

Saturday 31st May
A.M.

     No signals

P.M.

4.49 *To Van Squadron*
     PREPARE TO ENGAGE ENEMY'S VAN

4.57 *To Centre Squadron*
     PREPARE TO ENGAGE ENEMY'S CENTRE

7.7   Flagship hailed *Southampton* and desired Captain Forbes to inform the port division that the Admiral intended to carry the same sail, weather permitting, all night, letting as many reefs out of the topsails as possible without endangering the masts.

Sunday 1st June

A.M.

4.00   Fresh breezes and cloudy. Fleet in company, visible from Flagship.

6.00   Flagship counted 26 Enemy line-of-battle ships, 12 ahead and 13 astern of French Admiral, and 6 frigates.

8.00   Enemy Fleet NW to NE 4 miles from Flagship.
At the appropriate moment the Fleet then turned away from the wind and bore down on the enemy, singling out their adversaries. Many private signals were interchanged, for, junior Captains seemed to get in the way of their Seniors, and it was the first time in history the Seniors could tell them so by signal.
Once more *Queen Charlotte* broke through the enemy line, this time supported by most ships, except *Caesar*; throwing the Enemy into confusion. At about 9.30 intense fighting

5.14   *To Rear Squadron*
       PREPARE TO ENGAGE ENEMY'S REAR

6.27   *To Latona and Southampton (Frigate)*
       PASS WITHIN HAIL

6.34   *General*
       EACH SHIP TO CARRY A LIGHT THE ENSUING NIGHT AND
       REPEAT SIGNALS MADE BY THE ADMIRAL

7.13   *General*
       SHIPS ASTERN MAKE MORE SAIL

Sunday 1st June
A.M.

4.10   *General*
       CENTRE DIVISION TO KEEP IN CLOSER ORDER OF SAILING

4.13   *From Latona*
       ESTIMATE ENEMY'S FLEET 33 SAIL

5.00   *General*
       ALTER COURSE TO NORTH WEST

7.16   *General*
       FORM IN ORDER OF BATTLE

7.35   *General*
       INTEND TO PASS THROUGH THE ENEMY'S LINE AND ENGAGE
       THEM TO LEEWARD

started at close quarters. In luffing up alongside the French Admiral, *Queen Charlotte* lost her fore topmast and promptly dismasted an Enemy ship. *Brunswick's* duel with *Vengeur*, with anchors hooked, lasted four hours, after which *Vengeur* struck her Colours, drifted clear and sank.

P.M.

12.50 *Queen* hailed *Pegasus* and desired Captain Barlow to take her in tow.
By about 1 o'clock there were 12 dismasted ships in sight. *Marlborough*, *Defence*, and 10 Enemy ships.

3.00 Action ceased, enemy having had enough. Damage to

8.38 *General*
EACH SHIP TO STEER INDEPENDENTLY FOR AND ENGAGE HER
OPPONENT IN THE ENEMY'S LINE

8.55 *To Marlborough and Caesar*
MAKE MORE SAIL

9.12 *To Brunswick, Gibraltar, Culloden*
MAKE MORE SAIL

9.32 *General*
ENGAGE THE ENEMY CLOSER

9.40 *General*
MAKE MORE SAIL

10.00 *To Gibraltar and Culloden*
MAKE MORE SAIL

10.20 *General*
CHASE

11.5 *General*
CLOSE ROUND ADMIRAL

11.25 *General*
FLEET FORM IN LINE OF BATTLE AHEAD AND ASTERN OF THE
ADMIRAL AS CONVENIENT

11.45 *From Queen*
AM NOW IN CONDITION TO RENEW ACTION

P.M.

12.35 *From Defence*
REQUIRE ASSISTANCE

2.30 *From Brunswick*
INABILITY

masts, sails and rigging of our ships was extensive. Flagship lost fore and main topsail yards, topmasts and spritsail, much rigging and all signal halyards. Somehow or other the Enemy managed to tow away 4 or 5 disabled ships.

4.22   Took possession of seven Enemy ships.
       Enemy making off to leeward shattered and disabled.

8.00   Enemy Fleet out of sight.
10.00 Course of British Fleet ENE. Light airs. Prizes in tow.

Monday 2nd June
A.M. Shifted prisoners in frigates and boats and repaired damage. Most ships in their stations.

Noon Course North. S 86° W, 420 miles from Ushant.

The signals made and received on 29th May and 1st June indicate that the Commander-in-Chief was not satisfied with the way H.M.S. *Caesar* was handled, after having outsailed everyone in the long beat up to windward on 29th.

In April, 1795, her Captain was tried by Court Martial and dismissed his ship for not having done his utmost to bring his ship into close action with the enemy on those two days.

The Battle is summarised in a more domestic report from an

3.33 *General*
      KEEP IN THE ADMIRAL'S WAKE

3.52 *General*
      LEAVE OFF CHASE

4.15 *General*
      STAY BY PRIZES

4.50 *From Caesar*
      UNABLE TO STAY BY PRIZES

6.00 *To Caesar*
      ARE YOU IN CONDITION TO TAKE SHIP IN TOW

Monday 2nd June

A.M.

8.50 *General*
      FLEET CLOSE ROUND ADMIRAL

10.45 *General*
      BRING TO IN SUCCESSION, STERNMOST SHIP FIRST

Officer in the Queen's Regiment, written on board *Royal George* (100 guns) on 2nd June:

"Dear Mother,—After a smart and most decisive action we have, thank God, gained one of the most splendid victories ever fought at sea. The French fought with desperate bravery. We have taken six sail of-the-line; a three-decker was likewise taken on Wednesday last. Two French three-deckers and a seventy-four were towed off by their fleet dismasted, but we hope to catch them before they can gain Brest. Our ship and the *Queen* are greatly distinguished and much damaged. I am quite untouched. Our foremast and main and mizen topmasts are gone. The *Queen Charlotte's* main and fore topmasts are gone. Admirals Graves, Bowyer, and Pasley are wounded, Captain Montague killed. Lord Howe is safe. It was a desperate business and the victory was gained by our breaking the line. The *Royal George* went through first. You must understand that there have been two actions; one on the 29th May in which we were in the van and suffered much; another on 1st June, when we were in the rear. The first was only partial, the last decisive. We are now 150 leagues to the west of Ushant, but are returning home as fast as our shattered condition permits, etc., etc."

(Navy Records Society, 1899.)

THE BATTLE OF COPENHAGEN
2nd April, 1801

When Denmark joined Russia and Sweden in an armed neutrality against us, the Baltic was sealed.

Early in 1801 Britain decided that this seal must be broken, and on 7th March a Fleet of some 50 sail left Yarmouth for the Kattegat. Admiral Sir Hyde Parker commanded the Fleet with Vice Admiral Lord Nelson as second in command.

Delayed by gales the Fleet eventually arrived off Elsinore on 24th March. Terms were offered to the Danes which were promptly rejected. When Sir Hyde Parker sought to enter the sound the Governor of Elsinore regretted that "he was not at liberty to suffer such a fleet—whose intention was unknown—to pass."

This we regarded as an act of war, and on 30th March the Fleet weighed and Nelson, flying his flag in H.M.S. *Elephant*, took station in the van. Our ships passed out of range of an uninterrupted bombardment from the guns of Kronenburg Castle, and anchored about 10 miles from Copenhagen.

The Danes, meanwhile, were taking full measures to defend their capital. They removed the channel buoys, and built up a formidable defence of moored ships and floating batteries.

After inspecting these defences the C.-in-C. held a council of war on board H.M.S. *London*, his Flagship, on the afternoon of 31st March.

Nelson favoured immediate action. He paced the cabin "mortified at all remarks about intervention by Russia or Sweden which savoured of alarm or irresolution." He calmed down when he was given command of the Attacking Squadron. Sir Hyde Parker allowed him twelve line-of-battle ships and all available small craft.

By dark that evening the British pilots had replaced the channel buoys and the Attacking Squadron had moved in. By 1 a.m. the following morning Nelson's detailed operation orders were complete.

Narrative

2nd April 1801
A.M.

10.5   *Edgar* weighed and led the Squadron to the attack of the Danish line.
     Agamemnon grounded on middle. *Russell* and *Bellona* also grounded on shoal, within range of enemy.

10.40 *London* observed southern batteries open fire on *Edgar*. The ships of the Squadron followed in succession and anchored and opened fire as they arrived on their stations.

The events which took place and the signals which were made that day are taken from the logs of H.M. ships *London* and *Elephant*.

Signals

2nd *April* 1801
A.M.

7.15 *From Elephant to attacking Squadron*
CAPTAINS REPAIR ON BOARD FLAGSHIP

7.45 *From Elephant to attacking Squadron*
PREPARE FOR BATTLE

7.57 *From Elephant to attacking Squadron*
ARTILLERY OFFICERS REPAIR ON BOARD FLAGSHIP

9.00 *From Elephant General*
ARMED BARGES AND PINNACES PROCEED TO FLAGSHIP

9.10 *From London General*
MEN INTENDED TO BE LANDED ARE TO BE HELD IN READINESS TO LAND

10.00 *From Elephant to attacking Squadron*
WEIGH

10.20 *From London to Agememnon*
WEIGH

10.53 *From Elephant to attacking Squadron*
ENGAGE THE ENEMY MORE CLOSELY

11.30 *From Bellona*
AM STUCK ON A SHOAL

11.40 *From Bellona*
REQUIRE ASSISTANCE

P.M.

2.00   General Battle raged at close range. The greater part of the enemy line, being subdued, ceased fire. *Dannesbrog* (Danish flagship) struck her colours and later blew up. Lord Nelson sent a Flag of Truce to the Danish Government to arrange the landing of wounded prisoners. His Lordship's terms were accepted and all firing ceased.

3.15   Flag of Truce flying in *Elephant* observed from *London*.

4.00   *Elephant* cut cables and made sail for the outer harbour.

4.10   *Elephant* grounded on shoal.

9.30   *Elephant* refloated and rejoined fleet.
    The Danes then agreed to grant maintenance facilities and our Fleet proceeded into the Baltic.

The situation at noon from the Commander-in-Chief's point of view was gloomy. The *Agamemnon* was hard and fast on the middle ground flying the signal of inability. Distress signals flew from *Bellona* and *Russell*, also grounded. Only three out of the fourteen gun brigs and bomb vessels had managed to get into position. Our ships seemed to be getting better than they gave. The strong current which prevented the smaller craft getting into position also prevented him joining the Attacking Squadron. With the enemy always able to reinforce, the odds seemed to be against his second-in-command, and there was nothing he could do to help.

He therefore hoisted signal No. 39.

DISCONTINUE THE ENGAGEMENT

On board *Elephant*, Nelson had been pacing the quarterdeck since the action began. He was tense and alert. When a few splinters fell from the mainmast he remarked to those around him, "It is warm work, and this day may be the last to any of us

62

P.M.

12.15 *From London to Elephant*
DISCONTINUE THE ENGAGEMENT

---

at a moment, but I wouldn't be elsewhere for thousands."

At that moment the signal lieutenant reported the Commander-in-Chief's signal to him. At first he did not appear to take any notice. When the signal officer asked if he should repeat the signal he answered, "No, acknowledge it." As the officer returned to the poop, Nelson asked, "Is No. 16 still flying?" The officer answering in the affirmative, Nelson said, "Mind you keep it so." (No. 16 was the signal for close action hoisted at 10.53.)

The Admiral then became agitated, which he always showed by moving the stump of his right arm. After a turn or two he said, "Do you know what is shown on board of the Commander-in-Chief—No. 39? Why, it's leave off action. Leave off action," he repeated. "Now damn me if I do." Then turning to his Flag Captain, "You know, Foley, I have only one eye, I have a right to be blind sometimes." Putting his telescope to his blind eye he exclaimed, "I really do not see the signal."

So signal No. 39 was received and acknowledged, but it was never repeated to the Attacking Squadron.

NELSON'S SIGNAL AT TRAFALGAR
21st October, 1805

About fifteen months before the Battle of Trafalgar the signal book became compromised. *Redbridge*, a frigate commanded by Lieutenant Lempière, was captured by some French frigates off Toulon. Confidential signal books were not supplied to lieutenants, but Lempière had his own hand-painted edition which he failed to throw overboard when captured. When one of Nelson's scouts looked into Toulon later, she was told by signal from *Redbridge* to anchor. Fortunately the commanding officer was quicker witted than Lempière, and he hastened back to report the matter to his Admiral. Nelson told the Admiralty that the code had been compromised, and on 4th November, 1803, Their Lordships directed all C.'s-in-C. to alter their numeral flags in accordance with a painted copy enclosed. They also frowned heavily on all junior officers who made manuscript copies of secret documents. They still do.

The amended signals were in use at the Battle of Trafalgar. It was from them that the message of exhortation, which was to become the most famous signal in our Naval history, was made.

Lieutenant Pasco, signal officer to Lord Nelson in H.M.S. *Victory*, describes this occasion on the morning of Trafalgar, in a letter written after the battle.

"His lordship came to me on the poop, and after ordering certain signals to be made, about a quarter to noon he said, Mr Pasco, I wish to say to the Fleet, 'England confides that every man will do his duty,' and he added, 'You must be quick for I have one more to make which is for Close Action.' I replied, 'If your Lordship will permit me to substitute "Expects" for "Confides" the signal will soon be completed, because the word "Expects" is in the vocabulary and "Confides" must be spelt.' His Lordship replied in haste and with seeming satisfaction, 'That will do, Pasco. Make it directly.' "

The word "Duty" was also missing from the vocabulary and had to be spelt. While it seems strange that "Duty" was not included, there is no intention here to improve upon the selection of the 1,000 words which an admiral would find most useful.

And so, but for the change of one word, the signal was read by all ships present in a matter of minutes from the time Nelson composed it. Had he wished to send it six years before Trafalgar it would have had to be circulated by voice trumpet or boat.

One previous signal had already been sent that morning by Nelson, "Prepare to anchor after the close of day." As the 33 flags which made up the famous message were hoisted, Collingwood, Nelson's second in command, showed his distaste for any form of signal verbiage by exclaiming, "I wish Nelson would make no more signals, we all understand what we have to do." Later on, however, when he was shown the immortal words he repented with, "Great man, I forgive him."

To continue from Pasco's letter—No sooner had this signal been answered by a few ships in the van than, "he ordered me to make the signal for close action and to keep it up, accordingly I hoisted No. 16 at the top gallant masthead, and there it remained until shot away."

These three signals from the flagship, and the sixty or so others made by lookout vessels reporting enemy movements that day, show an interesting comparison with the number of signals made in the next major action which our Navy fought. In a four-hour period during the Battle of Jutland in 1916, 257 signals were made.

Nelson's signal at Trafalgar has been hoisted annually on board H.M.S. *Victory* on the anniversary of the Battle of Trafalgar ever since she sailed into Portsmouth Harbour for the last time. At first it was hoisted by men who had fought in the ship and knew the flags by heart; but, after some years, someone who knew nothing of the *Redbridge* incident said the flags were wrong, and they were changed. For the next twenty-three years the signal was hoisted incorrectly. In 1908 the mistake was discovered and rectified, but there is still some doubt about one of the flags.

MEDITERRANEAN MANŒUVRES
1893

On a bright sunny Mediterranean afternoon in June, 1893, in clear, calm weather, two battleships of the world's crack fleet were leading their respective divisions at nine knots on parallel courses, prior to anchoring off the port of Tripoli. One of these battleships, H.M.S. *Victoria*, flew the flag of Admiral Sir George Tryon, K.C.B., Commander-in-Chief of the Mediterranean fleet. Leading the port line was H.M.S. *Camperdown*, temporarily flying the flag of Rear Admiral A. H. Markham, Admiral Tryon's second in command.

At 3.27 *Victoria* hoisted a signal ordering the two divisions to turn towards one another. *Camperdown* hesitated, then made her turn and about four minutes later she struck *Victoria* on her starboard bow almost at right angles. At 3.44 *Victoria* sank, drowning Admiral Tryon, 22 officers and 336 men.

The Admiral was a tall, burly figure of a man with a masterful personality. He had seen war service in the Crimea and he had proved his ability at the Admiralty. With plenty of practical experience behind him, he had a flare for handling ships. He enjoyed carrying out complicated manœuvres. That very morning, on sailing from Beyrout, he had surprised his captains with a brilliant manœuvre which depended upon his judgment and timing. He was undoubtedly in every way suited to this important Command.

About noon on this ill-fated day he decided to anchor the fleet off Tripoli at 4 p.m. in a particular formation. Shortly after noon he signalled this formation so that all ships would know how and where they would finish up.

At 2.20 he formed the fleet into two divisions. Captains probably began to speculate with their officers as to how their Admiral would manœuvre them to arrive at the anchorage in that particular formation. They knew it would be neatly done. It always was with Admiral Tryon.

A certain detail was, however, puzzling at least one Captain. At the subsequent Court Martial, Captain Noel, of H.M.S. *Nile*, stationed astern of *Victoria*, said:

"As a rule, after the anchoring signal has been made, I have always found that I could foretell how the fleet was to be got into the necessary formation for anchoring. On the fatal 22nd June, 1893, the anchoring signal was made soon after noon. About half past two the columns were closed to six cables (1,200 yd.). It then occurred to me that there was some error, and we might have taken it wrong, so at 2.55, I made a signal, 'Please repeat third hoist of anchoring signal.' This was done, repeating the former signal. I still thought there was something wrong, but of course it was impossible for me to say where the mistake might have been."

There was, indeed, something very wrong.

The ships present were not all of one class. They varied in size and shape,—and consequently in turning power. To ensure uniformity in manœuvre, it was necessary for all ships to use such helm as would make their turning circles equal; that is, equal to the ship with the largest turning circle, which was about 800 yd. diameter.

To Captain Noel a solution to the problem would be for the leading ships of divisions to turn inwards 16 points (180 degrees) and, when this was completed, for all ships to turn together towards the anchorage. This would be simple if the divisions were more than twice their turning diameter apart—but six cables was not enough. At six cables their turning circles would overlap.

Before stationing the divisions at six cables the C.-in-C. had discussed the matter in his cabin with his Staff Commander and his Flag Captain. On explaining his intention the Staff Commander suggested that eight cables would be a better distance apart than six, to which the Admiral replies, "Yes, it should be eight cables." When the signal was hoisted however the Staff Commander (who survived the tragedy) noted the distance given was six cables, so he sent the Flag-lieutenant down to the Admiral to have it corrected.

The Captain (who also survived) was with the Admiral when the Flag-lieutenant entered. The Admiral now said the distance was to remain at six cables. At the Court Martial, the Captain said, "After the Flag-lieutenant left, I reminded the Commander-in-Chief that our turning circle was 800 yards. The interview I am referring to did not take more than a minute. To the best of my belief the Commander-in-Chief said to me, rather shortly, something to the effect of 'that's all right, leave it at six cables,' and then I left the cabin."

At 3.27, when the Commander-in-Chief, Captain, Staff Commander and Flag-lieutenant were on top of *Victoria's* chart house the Flag-lieutenant was ordered to hoist two signals—one to each division—ordering it to turn in succession 180 degrees inwards, towards its opposite division.

It did not take the Captains long to work out that the manœuvre they were being called upon to perform was dangerous, yet every ship except one acknowledged these signals, indicating that they were both seen and understood.

That one ship was *Camperdown*. When the signal was reported to Admiral Markham, he said at once, "It's impossible. It's an impracticable manœuvre," and directed his Flag-lieutenant to keep the repeat hoist "at the dip" indicating that the signal had been seen, but was not understood. He then made to the Commander-in-Chief by semaphore.

DO YOU WISH THE EVOLUTION TO BE PERFORMED AS INDICATED BY SIGNAL

But before this message got through, *Victoria* signalled to *Camperdown*,

WHAT ARE YOU WAITING FOR

Markham was no yes-man, but he readily acknowledged his Chief as his superior in manœuvre. He had followed him blindly before now. Besides, he thought, with these two separate hoists the divisions could be turned one at a time. Relieved at seeing a solution and not wishing to hold the fleet up any longer, Admiral Markham added his testimony that he understood the signal, and round went the two leaders.

When this incredible blunder eventually dawned on Admiral Tryon he stood, speechless, watching *Camperdown* approaching, heedless of the repeated urges of his Flag Captain to take avoiding action. After the collision he was heard to mutter "It's all my doing—all my fault," later he said to his Staff Commander, "I think she's going," and his last recorded words were to a midshipman, "Don't stop here, youngster—go to a boat."

The two signals hoisted by the Fleet Flagship at 3.27 were:

FIRST DIVISION ALTER COURSE IN SUCCESSION 16 POINTS TO PORT PRESERVING THE ORDER OF THE DIVISION.

SECOND DIVISION ALTER COURSE IN SUCCESSION 16 POINTS TO STARBOARD PRESERVING THE ORDER OF THE DIVISION.

(16 points is 180 degrees.)

The orders they conveyed were dangerous to every ship. Everyone trusted the leader, and his personality was such that his own officers and the Captains of other ships preferred to believe he had some trick up his sleeve than to challenge him on a matter of elementary arithmetic.

SHORT WEEK-END

In the winter months shortly before World War I Commodore Sir Robert Arbuthnot's destroyer flotilla was at Bantry Bay calibrating guns. Bad weather had considerably delayed the programme; in fact, his own ship had not even made a start. But the weather was improving and the experts prophesied that it would be possible to begin on Saturday. Unfortunately, they were twenty-four hours out in their reckoning and no guns could be fired that day; but Sunday held out still more promise.

The Gunnery Lieutenant asked the Staff Commander whether he could persuade the Admiral to allow firing to take place on the Sabbath. The Staff Commander, knowing Sir Robert pretty well, thought the Admiral would have no personal feelings on the matter, but said he would have to remind the Admiral about possible repercussions from the Roman Catholic population on shore.

The Admiral gave permission to go ahead with the plans to calibrate irrespective of the day of the week, but added cryptically that the guns would not be fired on a Sabbath day.

At one minute before midnight on Saturday, the Admiral made the following signal:

TOMORROW WILL BE MONDAY

Calibration went on uninterruptedly throughout daylight hours the following day.

At one minute past midnight on Monday morning, the Admiral signalled:

YESTERDAY WAS SUNDAY

Despite Episcopal protests from ashore and subsequent questions from the Admiralty, Sir Robert blandly maintained that no guns had been fired on the Sabbath.

A SIGNAL WHICH EXPLODED
1907

A signal made in Weymouth Bay in November, 1907, had almost the same effect as a spark in a petrol tank. The explosion which followed rumbled away for many years.

The detonation was caused by the conflicting temperaments of Admiral Lord Charles Beresford on one hand, and Admirals Fisher and Percy Scott on the other. Sir John Fisher was First Sea Lord, Lord Charles was Commander-in-Chief Channel Fleet. Rear Admiral Percy Scott was commanding a Cruiser Squadron.

Lord Charles was a nobleman. Sir John and Percy Scott were brilliant men whose creed at that time was Strength through Gunnery. All three had strong personalities.

The Channel Fleet was at Portland; the Cruisers in Weymouth Bay; Percy Scott flew his flag in H.M.S. *Good Hope*.

The Cruisers were carrying out their annual gunnery competitive firing, an affair of great importance to Percy Scott. Bad weather had held up the firing and by the end of the week when the competition should have been completed, one Cruiser, the *Roxburgh*, had not finished.

Kaiser William II was about to pay a State visit to this country and, at the end of the following week, the Fleet was to assemble at Spithead to greet him. This meant that all ships must look their smartest. Accordingly, the Commander-in-Chief had given orders that ships were to start painting on Monday.

On the previous Friday, Percy Scott asked the Commander-in-Chief if *Roxburgh* could go out in the Channel and complete her firing before she started painting on Monday.

Lord Charles made the following reply:

NOT APPROVED. ROXBURGH MUST GET READY FOR THE REVIEW AND REMAIN IN HARBOUR WITH THE REMAINDER OF THE FLEET.

Between Portland Harbour and Weymouth Bay, it was necessary to station a ship to repeat signals. H.M.S. *Illustrious*, flying the flag of Rear Admiral Foley was fulfilling this task. When *Illustrious* passed on the Commander-in-Chief's refusal to *Good Hope*, the explosion occurred.

When Percy Scott was shown the signal, he took a signal pad, and wrote. When his Flag Lieutenant saw what he had written he urged that the wording should be modified. The Flag Captain did the same. Their advice was scorned. The only concession the Admiral granted was to defer sending the signal until after lunch.

In desperation the Flag Lieutenant contacted his opposite number in *Illustrious*. Together they vowed they would do all they could to stop the signal being read by the Fleet. But after lunch the signal was duly passed to *Roxburgh*. It read as follows:

SINCE PAINTWORK APPEARS TO BE MORE IMPORTANT THAN GUNNERY YOU MUST REMAIN IN HARBOUR AND MAKE YOURSELF LOOK PRETTY.

During the afternoon officers foregathered as usual afloat and ashore and by evening everyone in the Fleet was discussing *Good Hope's* signal to *Roxburgh*. They did not have to wait long for developments. In due course *Roxburgh* was ordered to send her signal log to the Fleet Flagship. Rear Admiral Percy Scott was ordered to put on his frock coat and sword and personally to bring *Good Hope's* signal log to the Commander-in-Chief.

The C.-in-C. interviewed him on his quarter-deck before his staff and all the Captains of the Fleet. It must have been one of the most unpleasant sessions two Flag Officers have ever had. Having accepted the responsibility of making the signal, Percy Scott was told that the Admiralty had been requested to order him to haul down his flag. Percy Scott stated afterwards he was never given a chance to state his case. It seems that Lord Charles Beresford did all the talking.

Shortly after this distressing scene the following signal was made by semaphore to the whole fleet, thus ensuring the widest possible publicity.

From Commander-in-Chief—General.

THE LORDS COMMISSIONERS OF THE ADMIRALTY HAVING DIRECTED ME TO PREPARE THE CHANNEL FLEET TO DO HONOUR TO HIS IMPERIAL MAJESTY THE GERMAN EMPEROR AN ORDER WAS GIVEN TO ALL VESSELS UNDER MY COMMAND TO BE OUT

NAVAL HISTORY BY SIGNAL

OF ROUTING AND PAINT SHIP AFTER THE MANŒUVRES. WITH
REFERENCE TO MY ORDER ON MONDAY, 4TH NOVEMBER, THE
ADMIRAL COMMANDING THE FIRST CRUISER SQUADRON FORMING
PART OF THE CHANNEL FLEET MADE THE FOLLOWING SIGNAL TO
THE CAPTAIN OF THE ROXBURGH.
SINCE PAINTWORK APPEARS TO BE MORE IMPORTANT THAN
GUNNERY YOU MUST REMAIN IN HARBOUR AND MAKE YOURSELF
LOOK PRETTY.
IN REGARD TO MY ORDER MADE TO THE FLEET TO PAINT SHIP
THIS SIGNAL MADE BY THE REAR ADMIRAL FIRST CRUISER
SQUADRON IS CONTEMPTUOUS IN TONE AND INSUBORDINATE
IN CHARACTER. THE REAR ADMIRAL IS TO ISSUE ORDERS TO
GOOD HOPE AND ROXBURGH TO EXPUNGE THE SIGNAL FROM
THEIR SIGNAL LOGS AND TO REPORT TO ME BY SIGNAL WHEN
MY ORDERS HAVE BEEN OBEYED.

The episode certainly did not end there. Admiral Sir John
Fisher at the Admiralty, declined to order Percy Scott to strike
his flag on the grounds that the Commander-in-Chief had already
dealt with the matter by taking the unprecedented step of
censuring the Rear Admiral in a general signal to the whole
Fleet. This ruling showed clearly which side Sir John was on.

The incident didn't seem to affect the career of Percy Scott,
who finished his brilliant, if tactless career as a full Admiral and
a knight. The Battle, however, continued after retirement.

In 1912 Lord Charles Beresford wrote in his autobiography:

"It is now four years since I had occasion to appeal to the
Admiralty with reference to a grave instance of indiscipline in
which my authority as Commander-in-Chief and also my
personal character were involved. The matter having passed out
of my hands and having become known to the public at the time,
the Admiralty and the Admiralty alone could have set it right.

". . . During my tenure of the Command of the Channel
Fleet, two incidents occurred of which highly misleading accounts
appeared in the Press. The first occurred in November, 1907.
The breach of discipline was so grave a character and was committed in so public a manner that it was my duty to make strong

representations to the Admiralty with regard to the offender. Those representations were so far disregarded that the officer in question was permitted to retain his position without having proffered a public apology for a public offence.

"I appealed to the Admiralty in the interests of discipline to take such measures to put a stop to these nefarious proceedings as I was myself debarred by King's Regulations from adopting. The only response of the constituted authorities to my request was a brief statement made in the House on March 9th, 1908, many weeks after the event, by the Civil Lord of the Admiralty in answer to a question. By that time the mischief was done."

Here Lord Charles goes on to describe the second incident which, it relates, refers to a signal concerned with the manœuvring of *Good Hope* and *Argyll*. As Percy Scott did not leave *Good Hope* until January, 1909, it could well be related to the bitterness which still existed over the "Paint Ship" incident.

". . . In January, 1908, there was sent to every officer under my command in the Channel Fleet, a copy of a newspaper containing a violent attack upon myself.

"On Thursday, July 9th, an account of a signal said to have been made by me was published in the Press, together with a statement to the effect that had the signal been obeyed, a disaster comparable with the accident which befell the *Victoria* and the *Camperdown* must have occurred. The incident could only have been reported by an officer in the Fleet."

Lord Charles goes on to say that he showed the Civil Lord Mr. McKenna the written evidence in his possession with regard to the person who sent the account of the signal to the Press.

"On July 30th Mr McKenna said in the House that the signal was not dangerous, but that if the officer to whom the signal was made thought it was, he was quite justified in disobeying it. But . . . he had no knowledge who sent the message and it was impossible for him to find out."

In 1913 Sir Percy launched *his* attack. He maintained in *his* autobiography, that, "neither contempt nor insubordination was shown in my conversation with the Captain of the *Roxburgh*. Lord Charles publicly labelling it as such was a gross injustice to me and an act highly prejudicial to the maintenance of good order and discipline in H.M. Fleet. A further deplorable example to the officers and men under his command was Lord Charles Beresford's order to me not to speak to him, but only to communicate with him in writing. Such an act was extraordinary and fatal; it made him the laughing stock of the Fleet. . . . Such a state of affairs as the Commander-in-Chief of our Channel Fleet not to be on speaking terms with the Rear Admiral in Command of his Cruisers was nationally dangerous."

Then Sir Percy really warms up to his work. ". . . Lord Charles rightly says that a sailor can only learn his trade at sea, that his true education can only be gained at sea; the corollary of this is that if the sailor does not go to sea he can not learn his trade. In point of view of his education, I have always thought that the Admiralty treated Lord Charles very badly by not giving him sufficient opportunity at sea to acquire the necessary knowledge for establishing a reputation as a seaman. Out of the twenty-one years of his service in the Navy as Commander and Captain he only served in a ship of war for five years. This could not and did not make a seaman of him."

A POSSIBLE SOLUTION
1917

This incident contains a signal the text of which, as far as can be ascertained, has never been revealed. No mention is made of it at the Court of Inquiry which was held after the disaster. The incident is related here as it was told to the author.

"At the time in question I was serving as Signal Officer to Commodore (F) who commanded the five Destroyer Flotillas attached to the Grand Fleet. He flew his Broad Pennant in *Castor*.

"Attending the Destroyers was the *Sandhurst*. She was the largest Destroyer depot ship at that time. She was commanded by Captain English, a retired navigating officer recalled for the war. He had a fluent knowledge of the German language.

"*Sandhurst* was accommodating a number of Gunnery Artificers. They had been sent to carry out alterations to the magazines of certain ships. These alterations were found necessary after the explosions which sank three of our Battle Cruisers at the Battle of Jutland.

"I was walking up and down *Castor's* quarterdeck when at 11 p.m. precisely I saw *Vanguard* go up into the air in two quite distinct portions. It required no ballistical expert to realise that the explosion could have been the result of simultaneous time bombs.

"At daylight the next morning the following signal was received in *Castor*:

Captain of Sandhurst to Com. F.
AM SATISFIED I HAVE ARRESTED THE ENEMY AGENT RESPONSIBLE FOR BLOWING UP VANGUARD. WHEN MAY I COME AND SEE YOU.

"At the subsequent interview it transpired that on hearing the explosion, Captain English had promptly mustered every Gunnery Artificer on deck and had them brought down to his cabin one at a time.

"To each man he spoke—very slowly—a short sentence in German making him repeat it back as best he could. In three cases his suspicions were aroused. It seemed as though the ratings in question were familiar with the language, in spite of their assurance to the contrary.

"Captain English then turned up the history sheets of these three suspects. He noted that one had worked onboard *Bulwark* (previously sunk by explosion at Chatham) and onboard *Natal* (previously sunk by explosion at Cromarty). He had been onboard *Vanguard* up to 8 p.m. on the day she exploded.

"Later that morning I was ordered to detail one of the Duty Destroyers to take this Artificer under armed guard to Thurso. He went on by train to London to be interviewed by Admiral 'Blinker' Hall, the famous head of Naval Intelligence in World War I."

Nine months after this incident when the narrator was serving at the Admiralty he asked the Admiral what eventually happened to this Artificer. He was told politely to mind his own business.

V.I.S.
(VERY IMPORTANT SCIATICA)

A sequence of signals which passed between the Admiralty and the Commander-in-Chief, Grand Fleet, in World War 1.
All Private and Personal.

From First Lord of the Admiralty to Commander-in-Chief Grand Fleet

1650/17　I am sorry to learn you have sciatica. While the good information continues the Fleet and you should rest. Consider whether you should not take four or five days' holiday on shore at some comfortable Scotch house. We will take full responsibility for your absence. Keep fit it will last a long time.

1605/18　*From First Lord*
Pray let us know your wishes and make your own arrangements. We attach importance to your having a few days' holiday.

1058/27　*From Commander-in-Chief*
Medical Officer is very anxious for me to keep quiet for four days. If you consider it important to see me I will of course come.

1930/27 *From First Lord*
Your health and rest are first consideration. If possible I will come to you Friday night reaching you Saturday morning.

0905/28 *From First Sea Lord to Commander-in-Chief*
I earnestly entreat and urge you to take complete rest on shore as I can assure you that no present anxiety exists as to the Fleet being required and it is very urgent indeed you should completely re-establish your health by a long stay on shore without any Fleet work of any kind.

1050/28 *From Chief of Staff to Commander-in-Chief*
Request all Admiralty telegrams for Commander-in-Chief except personal telegrams may be repeated to Vice-Admiral Commanding 1st Battle Squadron until return of Commander-in-Chief.

1545/28 *From Commander-in-Chief to First Lord*
Doctors in consultation from Hospital Ship *Drina* today. They inform me it will be risky for me to be out of bed for four or five days. I am at Caledonian Hotel Inverness. Admiralty Mail Officer can decode telegrams sent to me direct. Much regret my temporary incapacity.

1843/28 *From Chief of Staff to Commander-in-Chief*
Doctor informs me it is essential Commander-in-Chief remains in bed for three or four days. I have informed Vice-Admiral Commanding 1st Battle Squadron. Submit I may be authorised to take Flagship to sea if such eventualities become necessary.

2340/28 *From First Sea Lord to Chief of Staff to Commander-in-Chief*
IMMEDIATE. Following has been sent to Vice-Admiral Commanding 1st Battle Squadron. In the event of Grand Fleet being required to proceed to sea during temporary indisposition of Commander-in-Chief you are authorised to take full command in his absence.

0915/30 *From First Lord*
Good to hear such favourable report. Inform C.-in-C. that there is nothing to cause him anxiety in anything that is occurring.

2157/1 *From Chief of Staff*
Doctor reports patient's condition most satisfactory. Could not be better.

1155/2 *From Chief of Staff to Medical Director General*
Patient thoroughly well and Doctors propose to go south at 3 p.m. today but if you think Sir . . . should wait he will do so for another day. On the other hand Sir . . . thinks it would be better for him to go now and return later in order to make sure that patient is all right before assuming duty.

1630/11 *From Chief of Staff to Medical Director General*
Patient is very anxious he should be allowed to attend to important correspondence and see his staff. Sir . . . considers this permissible for one hour daily. Meanwhile he has had another motor drive and is feeling much stronger.

1343/12 *From Medical Director General of the Navy to Chief of Staff*
One hour's work approved.

1915/17 *From Chief of Staff*
Doctor reports patient's convalescence. Steadily progressing. Yesterday and today he had been on board the Flagship transacting business. Tonight he is tired but well.

1845/19 *From Chief of Staff*
Doctor reports patient continues very well. He was on board Flagship four hours and afterwards played a round of golf.

1510/22 *From Commander-in-Chief to Admiralty*
I have returned to full duty. Ship will probably sail tomorrow afternoon.

SCHARNHORST AND GNEISENAU,
MUTTER UND TOCHTER

In the Naval history of the last two wars the names of *Scharnhorst* and *Gneisenau* are so closely associated that one would imagine the characters whose names they bear were twins. In historical fact Gerhard Johann David von Scharnhorst was five years older than August Wilhelm Anton Gneisenau. They had, however, many things in common. They were both eminent soldiers. They were both decorated with the envied *Pour le mérite*. Gneisenau actually worked under Scharnhorst in reforming the Prussian Army in 1809. Scharnhorst had Clausewitz as a pupil at the Berlin War Academy. Gneisenau had him later as his Chief of Staff. Scharnhorst was Chief of Staff to General Blücher after Napoleon's retreat from Moscow. Gneisenau was Blücher's Chief of Staff at Waterloo.

But the ships named after them seemed to be operationally inseparable.

In the World War 1 they were a couple of powerful cruisers completed in 1907, displacing 11,600 tons, with complements of 765 men, mounting 8 8·2 in. guns, 6 5·9 in. guns and capable of steaming 22 knots. They did not last long, but 88 of their 166 days of war life were spent at sea, covering 16,000 miles. With three light cruisers they inflicted at Coronel the first defeat the Royal Navy had suffered for over a century. It took a concentration of thirty ships to regain our command of the South Atlantic.

In World War 2 the daughters of *Scharnhorst* and *Gneisenau* were two mighty Battlecruisers displacing what they declared to be 26,000 tons but which we considered to be a modest underestimation of 10,000. They were armed with 9 11 in. guns, 85·9 in. and 16 4·1 in. They carried two aircraft and could steam 32 knots.

In company they sank the Armed Merchant cruiser *Rawalpindi*, and the aircraft carrier *Glorious* with her two destroyers *Acasta* and *Ardent*. For sixty days they evaded opposition in the Atlantic and between them they sank twenty-two merchant ships totalling 115,622 tons. A year later they shocked us by steaming up our Channel from Brest to their own dockyards.

There the partnership ended. Royal Air Force bombs put *Gneisenau* out of the war for good. *Scharnhorst* sailed for Norway once more and reached Altenfjord. In September, 1943, she ventured with *Tirpitz* on a one-sided raid on Spitzbergen. Finally she was pounced on and sunk by ships of the Home Fleet while threatening a Russian bound convoy on Boxing Day, 1943. By then her crew of about 1,900, substantially unchanged throughout the war, were a proud team with great faith in the fighting qualities of their ship.

One battleship, four cruisers and four destroyers were immediately responsible for their end, but the total sum of our ships ranged against these two in their lifetime must be unique.

Here is the story of those two *Scharnhorsts* and two *Gneisenaus* retold in the signals which shaped their lives.

World War I—Mutter

Scharnhorst was Admiral Graf von Spee's flagship on the China Station. With *Gneisenau*, her sister-ship, she had earned a great reputation for smartness and efficiency.

As the relationship between England and Germany became strained in the late summer of 1914, the movements of the two ships became of increasing interest to Vice Admiral Jerram, the British Commander-in-Chief on the China Station.

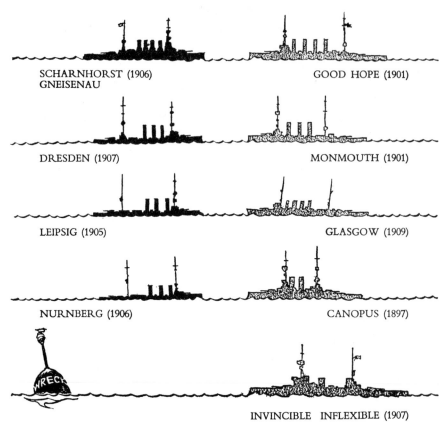

SCHARNHORST (1906)
GNEISENAU

GOOD HOPE (1901)

DRESDEN (1907)

MONMOUTH (1901)

LEIPSIG (1905)

GLASGOW (1909)

NURNBERG (1906)

CANOPUS (1897)

INVINCIBLE   INFLEXIBLE (1907)

On the eve of the outbreak of war, von Spee set out into the Pacific, never to return to the China seas.

In those days ships on distant foreign stations were not in direct wireless touch with London or Berlin. Long-distance communication was by cable, and messages were sometimes delayed.

October
1914
5th
From Admiralty to Rear Admiral Christopher Cradock, commanding 4th Cruiser Squadron in the Atlantic (Good Hope, flagship, Glasgow, Monmouth, Otranto, auxiliary cruiser, Canopus, old battleship).

It appears from information received that *Gneisenau* and *Scharnhorst* are working across to South America. *Dresden* may be scouting for them. You must be prepared to meet them in company. *Canopus* should accompany *Monmouth* and *Otranto* and should search and protect trade in combination.

8th
From Cradock to Admiralty (received 12th)
Without alarming, respectfully suggest that in event of enemy's heavy cruisers and others concentrating West Coast of South America it is necessary to have a British force on each coast strong enough to bring them to action. For otherwise, should the concentrated British force sent from South-East coast be evaded, which is not impossible, and thereby get behind the enemy, the latter could destroy Falkland, English Bank and Abrolhos coaling bases in turn with little to stop them, and with British ships unable to follow up owing to want of coal enemy might possibly reach West Indies.

8th
From Cradock to Admiralty (received 11th)
Following Intelligence re *Scharnhorst* and *Gneisenau* has been received. Evidence found by *Good Hope* revisiting Orange Bay on 7th October that *Dresden* had been there 11th and there are indications that *Scharnhorst* and *Gneisenau* may be joined by *Nurnberg, Dresden* and *Leipsig*. I have ordered *Canopus* to proceed there, and *Monmouth, Glasgow* and *Otranto* not to go further north than Valparaiso until German cruisers are located again. Does *Defence* join my command.

26th
From Cradock to Admiralty (received 27th)
With reference to orders to search for enemy and our great desire for early success, I consider that owing to slow speed of *Canopus* it is impossible to find and destroy enemy's squadron. Have therefore ordered *Defence* to

join me. . . . Shall employ *Canopus* on necessary work of convoying colliers.

27th   *From Cradock to Admiralty (received 1st November)*
Have seized German mails. *Monmouth, Good Hope, Otranto* coaling at Vallemar. *Glasgow* patrolling vicinity Coronel to intercept German shipping, rejoining flag later on. I intend to proceed northward secretly with squadron after coaling and to keep out of sight of land. Until further notice continue telegraphing to Montevideo.

27th   *From Rear Admiral Stoddart (East Coast) to Admiralty (arrived 29th)*
I have received orders from Admiral Cradock to send *Defence* to Montevideo . . . submit I may be given two cruisers in place of *Defence* as I do not consider force at my disposal is sufficient.

28th   *From Admiralty to Cradock*
Defence is to remain on East Coast under orders of Stoddart. This will leave sufficient force on each side in case the hostile cruisers appear there on the trade routes. . . . Japanese battleship *Hizen* shortly expected on North American Coast. She will join with Japanese cruiser *Idzumo* and *Newcastle*.

(This signal and subsequent signals sent from Admiralty to *Good Hope* were never received.)

Night   Frequent German wireless transmissions noted in
31/1   *Glasgow's* signal log.
Nov.
1st
0200   *From German Merchant ship Gottingen to Scharnhorst*
English light cruiser anchored in Coronel Roads 1900 31 October.

1620   *From Scharnhorst to ships in company*
Clear for action.

1628   *From Scharnhorst to Gneisenau*
Take station astern. Raise steam for full speed.

1647   *From Glasgow to Good Hope*
Enemy protected cruisers in sight steering between SE and South.

1818   *From Good Hope to Canopus (300 miles South)*
I am now going to attack enemy.

1834   *From Scharnhorst to Gneisenau*
Open fire.

1839   *From Good Hope to Otranto*
There is danger proceed at your utmost speed (message unfinished).

2015   *From Glasgow to Monmouth*
Are you all right.

       From Monmouth to Glasgow
I want to get stern to sea. I am making water badly forward.

       From Glasgow to Monmouth
Can you steer north west. The enemy are following us astern.

          (There was no answer from *Monmouth*).

Nov.   *From Consul General, Valparaiso to Admiralty (arrived 3rd)*
2nd   Master of Chilean merchant vessel reports that on 1st November 1 p.m. he was stopped by *Nurnberg* 5 miles off Cape Carranza. . . . Two other German cruisers lay west. . . . Master believes one of these was *Scharnhorst*. . . .

Nov.   *From Admiralty to Stoddart, Defence*
3rd   *Defence* to proceed with all possible dispatch to join Admiral Cradock on west coast of America. Acknowledge.

Nov.   *From Admiralty to Cradock*
3rd   *Defence* has been ordered to join your flag with all dispatch. *Glasgow* should find or keep in touch with the enemy. You should keep touch with *Glasgow* concentrating the rest of your squadron including *Canopus*. It is important you should effect your junction with

Defence at earliest possible moment subject to keeping touch with *Glasgow* and enemy. Enemy supposes you at Corcovados Bay. Acknowledge.

November 3rd. *Scharnhorst* sent full report of Coronel action to German Consul, Valparaiso, for onward transmission by cable to Naval Staff, Berlin, where it arrived on 6th November.

Nov. 3rd	*From Consul General Valparaiso, to Admiralty (arrived 4th)* Have just learnt from Chilean Admiral that German Admiral states that on Sunday at sunset, in thick and wicked weather his ships met *Good Hope, Glasgow, Monmouth* and *Otranto*. Action was joined and *Monmouth* turned over and sank after about an hour's fighting. *Good Hope, Glasgow* and *Otranto* drew off into darkness. *Good Hope* was on fire, an explosion was heard, and she is believed to have sunk. *Gneisenau, Scharnhorst* and *Nurnberg* were among the German ships engaged.
Nov. 4th	*From Admiralty to C.-in-C. Grand Fleet* Order *Invincible* and *Inflexible* to fill up with coal at once and proceed to Berehaven with all dispatch. They are urgently needed for foreign service. . . .
Nov. 4th	*From Admiralty to Kent (Sierra Leone)* Urgent. Proceed to Abrolhos Rocks with all dispatch. It is intended you shall join Admiral Cradock's Squadron.
Nov. 4th	*From Admiralty to Rear Admiral Stoddart (Carnarvon)* In view of reported sinking of *Good Hope* and *Monmouth* by *Scharnhorst* and *Gneisenau* off Coronel November 1st, armoured ships on SE coast of America must concentrate at once. *Carnarvon, Cornwall* should join *Defence* off Montevideo. *Canopus, Glasgow, Otranto* have been ordered if possible to join you there. *Kent* from Sierra Leone also has been ordered to join your flag via Abrolhos. Endeavour to get into communication with them. Enemy will most likely come on to the Rio trade route. Reinforcements will meet you shortly from England. Acknowledge.

Nov.
4th

*From German Naval Staff, Berlin to Von Spee (Scharn-
horst)*

*It is left to your discretion to attempt to return home with all
your ships.*

Nov.
4th

From Admiralty to Canopus

In view of reported sinking of *Good Hope* and *Monmouth*
by *Scharnhorst* and *Gneisenau* on 1st November you
should make the best of your way to join *Defence* near
Montevideo. Keep wide of track to avoid being brought
to action by superior force. If attacked, however,
Admiralty is confident ship will in all circumstances be
fought to the last as imperative to damage enemy
whatever may be consequences.

Nov.
4th

From Admiralty to Glasgow, Otranto

You should make the best of your way to join *Defence*
near Montevideo. Keep wide of track to avoid being
brought to action by superior force.

Nov.
5th

From Admiralty to Japanese Admiralty

In consequence of unsuccessful action off Chile and
definite location of German Squadron, we have ordered
concentration off Montevideo of *Defence, Kent, Carnarvon* and *Cornwall*. These will be joined with all
dispatch by *Inflexible* and *Invincible*, Battle cruisers from
England, and *Dartmouth*, light cruiser from East Africa,
and remainder of defeated squadron from Chile. This
assures the South Atlantic situation. We now desire
assistance of Japan in making equally thorough arrangements on Pacific side. We propose for your consideration and friendly advice the following. *Newcastle* and
Idzumo to go south in company to San Clemente
Island off San Diego, California, there to meet *Hizen*
from Honolulu. Meanwhile *Asama* will be able to effect
internment or destruction of *Geier*. We also propose to
move *Australia* battle cruiser from Fiji to Fanning
Island. By the time these moves are complete, probably
by November 17th we may know more of *Scharnhorst*
and *Gneisenau* movements, and a further concentration

of *Australia* and *Asama* with *Hizen, Idzumo* and *Newcastle* will be possible either at San Clemente or further to the south, further movements depending on the enemy. We should also like a Japanese Squadron to advance to Fiji to take the place of *Australia* and so guard Australia and New Zealand in case the Germans return. . . .

Nov. 5th
From Admiralty to C.-in-C. Grand Fleet (Personal from First Lord)
From all reports received through German sources, we fear Cradock has been caught or has engaged with only *Monmouth* and *Good Hope* against armoured ships *Scharnhorst* and *Gneisenau*. Probably both British vessels sunk. Position of *Canopus* critical and fate of *Glasgow* and *Otranto* uncertain. Proximity of concentrated squadron of five good ships will threaten gravely main trade route Rio to London. Essential recover control. Sturdee goes Commander-in-Chief, South Atlantic and Pacific.

Note:
Extract from orders to Vice Admiral Sturdee.
On leaving Devonport with H.M. ships *Invincible* and *Inflexible* under your orders proceed to St. Vincent, Cape Verde Islands and complete with coal on arrival there and thence proceed to South American waters.
On passage to St. Vincent it is possible you may receive orders by W/T to proceed to West Indies, should information be received that *Scharnhorst* and *Gneisenau* are proceeding northward on Pacific Coast. Your presence in the West Indies would be necessary to provide for the contingency of the German Squadron passing through the Panama Canal.
Your main and most important duty is to search for the German armoured cruisers *Scharnhorst* and *Gneisenau* and bring them to action. All other considerations are to be subordinated to this end.

Nov. 5th
From Admiralty to Governor, Falkland Islands
German cruiser raid may take place. All Admiralty colliers should be concealed in unfrequented harbours.

Be ready to destroy supplies useful to enemy and hide codes effectively on enemy ships being sighted. Acknowledge.

Nov.
7th

From Captain Von Knorr (German Naval attache San Francisco) to Von Spee (Scharnhorst)
Information received that British cruisers Defence, Cornwall, Bristol, Glasgow, Canopus assembling Falkland Islands. Japanese ships approaching from north on west coast. If it is your intention to return Germany suggest you do so now.

Nov.
7th

From Japanese Admiralty to Admiralty
Japanese Admiralty give their consent generally to strategical scheme proposed. . . .

Nov.
9th

From Admiralty to Canopus
You are to remain in Stanley Harbour. Moor the ship so that the entrance is commanded by your guns. Extemporize mines outside entrance. Send down your topmasts and be prepared for bombardment from outside the harbour. Stimulate the Governor to organize all local forces and make determined defence. Arrange observation posts on shore by which your fire on ships outside can be directed. Land guns or use boats' torpedoes to sink a blocking ship before she reaches the Narrows. No objection to your grounding ship to obtain a good berth. Should *Glasgow* be able to get sufficient start of enemy to avoid capture, send her to the River Plate, if not moor her inside *Canopus*. Repair your defects and wait orders.

Nov.
9th

From Commander-in-Chief, Plymouth to Admiralty
The Admiral Superintendent, Devonport, reports that the earliest possible date for completion of *Invincible* and *Inflexible* is midnight 13th November.

Nov.
9th

From Admiralty to C.-in-C. Plymouth
Ships are to sail Wednesday 11th. They are needed for war service and dockyard arrangements must be made to conform. If necessary dockyard men should be sent away in the ships to return as opportunity may offer.

You are held responsible for the speedy dispatch of these ships in a thoroughly efficient condition. Acknowledge.

Nov. 9th *From German Naval Staff, Berlin to German Consul, Valparaiso*
Instruct cruiser squadron that coaling from colliers in harbour Argentine and Brazil is not possible owing to embargo on coal export.

Nov. 16th *From German Naval Staff to Von Spee (Scharnhorst)*
What are your intentions. Report amount of ammunition remaining.

Nov. 16th *From Scharnhorst to German agents, River Plate and New York*
Send German ship with 10,000 tons coal and sufficient provision for 1,000 men for three months to arrive Panta Santa, Elena (Argentine coast) December 15th.

Nov. 17th *From Von Spee to German Naval Staff*
Intend breaking through with my squadron. Ammunition remaining Heavy class. Main armament 445, secondary armament 1,100. Smaller cruisers 1,860.

Nov. 18th *From Invincible to Inflexible*
0345 The utmost harm may be done by indiscreet use of wireless. The key is never to be pressed unless absolutely necessary.

November 20th. German Agents, La Plata, had information for Von Spee that *Canopus'* guns had been mounted ashore, Falkland Islands.

November 23rd. German Agents, Montevideo, had information for Von Spee that ten English ships had been sighted 300 miles east of Montevideo.

November 24th. German Agents, La Plata, had information for Von Spee that *Invincible* and *Carnarvon* were at Albrolhos Rocks.

(None of the above information ever reached Von Spee.)

Dec. 6th *From German ship Amasis to Von Spee (Scharnhorst)*
Naval base Port Stanley, Falkland Islands, empty of British warships.

Dec. 6th *From Port Stanley to Invincible*
1530   Following message received from Montevideo by W/T. Rio de Janeiro reports on 24th November there were rumours *Scharnhorst* and *Gneisenau* rounded Cape Horn 22 November.

Dec. 7th *From Sappers Hill (observation station, Falkland Island) to Canopus*
British battlecruisers approaching.

Extract from *Canopus'* signal log between 0700 and 0800 on Tuesday, 8th December.

0707   *From Ordnance Point to Canopus*
Submit is Yeoman Brooks still on compensation as there are 21 ratings here at present and rations for only 20 have been sent.
Reply: Brooks must be rationed additional. Rations for full numbers will be sent.

0750   *From Sappers Hill*
There is a four funnel and two funnel man of war coming from the southward.

0803/8 *From Invincible to Glasgow*
Where is Sappers Hill.

From Glasgow to Invincible
Sappers Hill is shore station above the town.

0805 *From Invincible to Glasgow, Cornwall*
Raise steam for full speed. Prepare to weigh.

0815 *From Invincible—General*
Raise steam for full speed and report when ready to proceed.

0830 *From Invincible—General*
Strange men-o'-war reported from southward. *Bristol* cast off collier and weigh immediately. Ships are to report when they have steam for 14 knots.

0935 *From Glasgow to Invincible*
There are three more cruisers in sight.

0945 *From Invincible to Glasgow*
Join *Kent* and observe enemy's movements.

1015 *From Invincible*
Follow Flagship out of harbour.

1030 *From Invincible—General*
CHASE.

1100 *From Bristol to Invincible*
Three enemy ships are standing off Port Pleasant. Probably colliers or transports.

1130 *From Invincible to Bristol*
Take *Macedonia* under your orders and destroy transports.

1140 *From Invincible—General*
Optional. Ship's companies will have time for the next meal.

1245 *From Scharnhorst*
Light cruisers detach and endeavour to escape.

1302 *From Invincible—General*
Open fire and engage enemy.

1545   *From Scharnhorst to Gneisenau*
        If engines are intact endeavour to escape.
        (This was the last signal from *Scharnhorst.*)

1830   *From Invincible—General*
        Scharnhorst and *Gneisenau* sunk. Where are the remainder.

Later   *From Invincible to Admiralty*
        Scharnhorst, Gneisenau, Leipsig sunk. 2 colliers captured.
        All cruisers now looking for *Dresden* and *Nurnberg* who
        spread and escaped during action.

Dec. 9th *From Admiral Sturdee to Senior surviving German Officer*
            from Gneisenau
        We sympathise with you in the loss of your Admiral
        and so many officers and men. Unfortunately the two
        countries are at war and officers of both navies who can
        count friends in the other have to carry out their
        country's duties, which your Admiral, Captain, and
        officers worthily maintained to the end.

1820/9 *From Canopus to Invincible*
        Message received from Admiralty through Monte-
        video begins: From His Majesty. I heartily congratulate
        you, your officers and men on your most opportune
        victory. George.

World War II—Tochter

Here starts the longer lives in the second world war of the two
descendants of Von Spee's squadron. They were launched in
October and December, 1936. *Gneisenau* lived for five-and-a-half
years. *Scharnhorst,* unlike the general she was named after,
survived *Gneisenau* by twenty months. Their first adventure after
the outbreak of war was a tame affair. They could have done
more damage than sinking one armed merchant cruiser and we
could possibly have brought them to action. Nevertheless the

German naval staff were extremely pleased that our northern sanctuaries had been penetrated without German loss so soon after the outbreak of war.

Sinking of H.M.S. RAWALPINDI (Armed Merchant Cruiser)

1325/21 Nov. 1939	*Gneisenau*, flying flag Admiral Marschall, with *Scharnhorst* in company sailed from Wilhelmshaven.
23rd Nov. 1605	*From Rawalpindi (on patrol between Faroes and Iceland)* 1 enemy Battle Cruiser bearing 280°, 4 miles. My position (given).
1607	*From Scharnhorst to Gneisenau* *Merchant ship at long range on starboard beam.*
1612	*From Gneisenau to Scharnhorst* *Ascertain course of Merchant ship. What type of vessel.*
1613	*From Scharnhorst to Gneisenau* *Merchant ship on roughly parallel course.*
1618	*From Scharnhorst to Gneisenau* *Am closing merchant ship to observe further details. Apparently a large ship. 2 masts one funnel.*
1624	*From Delhi (on northern patrol)* Am coming to your assistance.
1633	*From Scharnhorst to Gneisenau* *Large Merchant vessel, course 180°, vessel turning away. I am closing her.*
1635	*Scharnhorst to Rawalpindi* (In German) *Heave to. Do not use radio. Where from and where bound.* (In English) *What ship. Do not use wireless.*

Rawalpindi acknowledged the message, turned away and increased speed. *Scharnhorst* followed and noted a gun, mounted aft, and also that smoke floats were being dropped.

1655   *From Vice Admiral Northern Patrol to Cruisers*
Subject to other orders from Commander-in-Chief Home Fleet, *Delhi* and *Newcastle* shadow *Deutschland*. *Calypso*, *Ceres* concentrate 5 miles north of Kalso light. Act as striking force for night attack.

(Note: Identity of German ships was mistaken throughout. At this time *Deutschland* was in Kiel.)

1704. *Scharnhorst* opened fire on *Rawalpindi*. Range 4 miles.

1740   *From Gneisenau to Scharnhorst*
Close the enemy.

1745   *From Gneisenau to Scharnhorst*
Pick up 2 boatloads of survivors.

1746   *From Newcastle*
Gun flashes bearing 050° my position (given).

1750   *From Newcastle*
Ship indicated is on fire.

1815   *From Rawalpindi* (Ship is now blazing. Signal made from stern)
Please send boats.

1817   At 13,000 yards range *Newcastle* read the following from *Scharnhorst* made by flashlamp:
UM UM GO GO FOLGEN.

1819   *From Newcastle*
2 unknown vessels bearing 060°, 6 miles, course unknown, position (given).

1821   *From C.-in-C. Home Fleet to Newcastle*
Your 1746. *Rawalpindi* is in action with German armoured ship of *Deutschland* class.

1900   *From Newcastle*
My 1819. Vessels were hostile. Have lost touch.

1912   *From Gneisenau to Scharnhorst*
How long do you require to pick up survivors. Make all haste.

1913   *From Scharnhorst to Gneisenau*
        About 15 minutes.

1914   *From Gneisenau to Scharnhorst*
        Cease picking up survivors immediately. Follow Gneisenau.

1920   *From Scharnhorst to Gneisenau*
        Vessel bearing 150° showing no lights.

1932   *From Gneisenau to Scharnhorst*
        Make smoke.

1934   *From C.-in-C. Home Fleet to Newcastle*
        Your 1900. Consider that German armoured ship
        Deutschland class is homeward bound. Make every
        endeavour to regain touch.

1937   *From Scharnhorst to Gneisenau*
        Unknown vessel no longer in sight.

1959   *From Scharnhorst to Gneisenau*
        *Prisoners state sunken enemy ship was merchant cruiser
        Rawalpindi, armament 8 6-in. guns, 2 A.A. guns. Crew
        approximately 700 men. Scharnhorst hit on quarter deck
        but deck not penetrated.*

2005   *From Newcastle*
        Nothing in sight, my position (given).

1300/27 *Gneisenau* and *Scharnhorst* anchored Wilhelmshaven.

Sinking of GLORIOUS
8th June 1940

In early June, 1940, the two battlecruisers were at sea again with
Admiral Marschall flying his flag in *Gneisenau*. This time they
were accompanied by *Hipper* and four destroyers and they were
on a more ambitious mission. If the admiral had obeyed his
orders to attack Harstadt, our Norwegian base, there is no
knowing what they might have run into, for we were busy

evacuating at that time. But instead he decided to attack shipping, and on 8th June he and his force had quite a busy day.

At 0605 *Scharnhorst* sighted the tanker *Oil Pioneer*, escorted by the trawler *Juniper*. By 0717 the tanker and trawler were sinking. At 1002 their aircraft reported a transport (*Orama*) and a hospital ship (*Atlantis*). By 1206 *Orama* was sinking. The hospital ship was not molested. *Hipper* and the destroyers were then detached, and the redoubtable pair struck out towards Jan Mayen Island, in quest of a reported aircraft carrier.

Glorious at that time was proceeding home independently, escorted by destroyers *Acasta* and *Ardent*. *Veteran* and *Vanoc* were on their way from Harstadt to supplement the escort. One would imagine *Glorious* would have been flying a defensive air patrol but she was not. Everyone onboard was tired out after prolonged round-the-clock flying operations. She thought she was clear and safe. Beneath the smoke which *Scharnhorst* sighted at 1700 probably about 70 per cent of the officers and men were asleep. The German plan to close quickly and disable the flight deck before aircraft could be flown off was successful. From the start *Glorious* never had a hope. The action cost the German battle-cruisers a mere 400 rounds of ammunition, and two hours of their time.

The two destroyers fought back magnificently. The Germans were amazed at their courage. *Ardent* shielded *Glorious* for a while by laying a smoke screen, *Acasta* closed and attacked *Scharnhorst* and scored a fine torpedo hit which was to put her out of action for several months. The bravery of those two captains, especially *Acasta's*, was of the highest. One still wonders why it was never officially recognised.

At 1808 Admiral Marschall had signalled to Gruppe North:

ENEMY AIRCRAFT CARRIER IN POSITION (GIVEN) PROCEEDING AT FULL SPEED ON A SOUTH EASTERLY COURSE.

With wireless telegraphy as it was at that time, news of an engagement should have reached the authorities while it was in progress or soon afterwards. The tragedy of the *Glorious* was an exception. Our first official report of the engagement was passed to Commander-in-Chief Home Fleet from hand to hand a week or so later, as it might have been brought by a frigate in the days before wireless was thought of.

When *Scharnhorst* and *Gneisenau* had replied to *Ardent's* signal challenge with salvoes of 11 in., an enemy report was immediately initiated by *Glorious's* Captain. An aircraft carrier is a network of wireless installations and aerials. With all this equipment available, however, the Warrant Telegraphist who was handling this signal and trying to get it away, soon found himself in a race with the German gunners. Wherever he turned the apparatus was smashed by enemy shells.

No signal was sent by either of the destroyers. Whenever an enemy was sighted simultaneously by destroyer and big ship, it was conventional in those days for the big ship to make the reporting signal. No allowance was made for the big ship not being able to do so.

As the situation in *Glorious* became desperate, the Warrant Telegraphist fell back on an improvised wireless set rigged on the bridge for the purpose of communicating with aircraft. It was the last hope. Believing that the first reporting signal had been sent and that it would have been read (which, sad to say was not the case) he managed to send this amplifying report:

MY 1615. TWO POCKET BATTLESHIPS

This signal was read by only one ship, and that ship unfortunately could neither retransmit it nor act upon it. The cruiser *Devonshire* received it at 1720. She had sailed the previous day from Tromso for England with the King of Norway on board. She was therefore keeping strict wireless silence and could only hope that someone else had read it as well.

Returning to the *Atlantis*: in return for not being attacked, she had played her international part as a hospital ship by not reporting the enemy by wireless. She remained silent until contacted by the battleship *Valiant* the following day. So by the time it was safe for *Devonshire* to pass on the brief signal from *Glorious*, the evidence we had was: this brief signal, the report from *Atlantis* to *Valiant*, our inability to contact *Glorious* by wireless, and the German radio. The only British naval men who knew the full story were now struggling in the cold water on rafts and wreckage with their ships sunk deep beneath them.

Some of these survivors were picked up by a ship and taken to Norway where they became prisoners of war. About thirty others were found by another ship and taken to the Faroes. Here they were collected by *Veteran* and *Vanoc*, the destroyers who had been on their way to supplement *Glorious's* escort.

As the destroyers left the Faroes the weather was bright and sunny and arrangements were made for the survivors to recline on the upper deck. But no, they had had enough unrelieved daylight in the latitudes of the midnight sun. They had had 56 hours in the water, uncertain whether the enemy would return and find them. All they wanted now was food, warmth, some light music from the BBC and—darkness. The tragedy of the *Glorious* was extracted from them as they lay in the dark. By torchlight, notes were made from which a report was drawn up. As *Veteran* passed through the Pentland Skerries on her way to Rosyth this report was shot across by rocket gun-line to another destroyer waiting outside Scapa Flow. The second destroyer returned to the Fleet Flagship and so the grim facts were eventually placed before the Commander-in-Chief Home Fleet.

Five days previously *Scharnhorst* and *Gneisenau* had anchored peacefully in Trondheim.

This sortie marked a split between Admiral Marschall and his Commander-in-Chief, Admiral Raeder. Marschall's report on the operation was one long grumble about the risks he was forced to take and the inadequacy of his weapons. On one page of this report Rear Admiral Fricke, Chief of Naval Operations, writes in the margin "To hell! What is needed is a grasp of this new tactical role and a determination to take opportunities, if results are to be achieved."

Needless to say, Admiral Marschall did not remain in this command.

Operations in the Atlantic
22nd January–22nd March 1941

In the winter of 1940–41 the German naval staff supplemented their U-boats with surface ships. *Hipper* operated to the southward as one unit, and on the 28th December *Gneisenau* hoisted the flag of Admiral Lutjens and sailed with *Scharnhorst* to harass the north Atlantic convoy routes. They ran into exceptionally vicious weather off Norway which damaged *Gneisenau's* foc's'le beyond the resources of Norwegian dockyards, and back they came.

On 22nd January they set out once more from Kiel. The Admiral hoped to break through into the Atlantic south of Iceland but very soon he sensed that the Home Fleet was barring his way. On the night of 28th/29th in seasonable weather the Germans brushed against a line of cruisers, and were extremely lucky in managing to slip round them. These three signals show how lucky they were.

1445/28 *From C.-in-C. Home Fleet to Admiralty*
> Am discontinuing search. Intend to return to Scapa Flow with my force arriving a.m. 30 January if no further information is received.

Just as they were turning for home:

0140/29 *From Naiad to C.-in-C. Home Fleet*
> Am chasing two unknown ships approximate course 070°, my position (given).

The contact was lost and nothing further was reported. The C.-in-C. summed up as follows:

0027/31 *From C.-in-C. Home Fleet to Admiralty*
> Investigation of (*Naiad's*) report of sighting unknown ships produces evidence that is far from conclusive.

Snow squalls made visibility and Radar conditions patchy and liable to be misleading. There is a small possibility that, if a fast enemy vessel was present she could have worked round to northward and then to westward without being detected. I consider it unlikely that an enemy ship was present.

There was no doubt about the contact with *Naiad* in Admiral Lutjens' mind. His summing up was that either they had not been seen or they would run into stronger opposition concentrated ahead. It was a great relief therefore when they found a hole in the ice and in their opponents' defences, through the Denmark Strait twenty miles from the coast of Iceland. At noon on 3rd February the Admiral expressed his relief in this signal:

> *For the first time in the history of German warfare German battleships have succeeded in safely breaking through to the Atlantic. Go to it.*

Later that day they had additional reassurance that they had not been spotted breaking through.

2217/3   *From Gruppe North*
Air reconnaissance of Scapa Flow at 1530 shows following ships present. 7 battleships and heavy cruisers, 4 light cruisers.

Having fuelled from their auxiliaries south of Greenland they turned their attention to the northern convoy route on which vital war material was passing in the big HX convoys from Halifax to England. They did not have to wait long.

0835/8   *From Gneisenau to Scharnhorst*
Convoy in sight (position given) probably HX 108 (it was HX 106).

0841   *From Gneisenau to Scharnhorst*
Enemy steering 045°. Intend to attack from the south. Expect you to attack from the north at 1030.

0928   *From Scharnhorst*
One battleship Ramillies class (position given).

0947   *From Gneisenau*
Break off engagement taking avoiding action to southward.
Assemble (position given astern of the convoy).

1050/8   *From Ramillies to Admiralty*
At 1000 in position (given) had brief glimpse of mast
and top of warship possibly German *Hipper* class. . . .

When *Gneisenau* and *Scharnhorst* met astern of the convoy the
Admiral learnt that *Scharnhorst* had deliberately shown herself to
Ramillies in the hope of drawing her away from the convoy and
leaving it on a plate for *Gneisenau*. This was not at all according
to the Admiral's plan—a fact which he expressed in some heated
visual signals which unfortunately are not recorded. The Admiral
knew the British could not afford a battleship with every convoy.
He therefore decided to leave HX 106 well alone, without revealing his presence, and wait for the next. *Scharnhorst* had spoilt the
whole thing. Gruppe West would have to be told. Breaking
wireless silence on this sort of operation was an unpleasant risk
but now it had to be accepted.

0800/9   *From Gneisenau to Gruppe West*
Operation has been identified by the enemy.

Gruppe West acted on this by throwing out a hint to *Hipper*
who was operating against our Atlantic trade further south.

0100/10   *Gruppe West to Hipper*
Gneisenau reports operation has been identified by the enemy
Hipper now able to operate.

Hipper interpreted this correctly as a suggestion that she should
cause a diversion in her area.

      From Hipper
Have attacked convoy south east of Azores. 13 ships sunk.
Returning to Brest. Expect to arrive 14 February.

This was splendid news for Lutjens. If only another less heavily
escorted HX convoy would turn up. But he saw nothing except
one or two independently routed ships which he sank.

Gneisenau again broke wireless silence, this time with short transmissions at short intervals. In these signals she told Gruppe West that no convoy had appeared since the heavily guarded HX 106 fourteen days ago. She added that their oiler had not turned up at the appointed rendezvous, and that they were running short of fuel. Also that the score, to date, was 25,000 tons of shipping sunk. To dispel any feeling of disappointment in his Squadron the Admiral handed out a bouquet:

27/2   *From Admiral Lutjens*
         Battleships have covered in this operation up to now over 11,000 miles which is equal to half way round the world. I express my full appreciation to the engine room personnel of my battleships for this record efficiency.

But the area was not productive enough, and the Admiral decided to move.

28/2   *From Gneisenau to Gruppe West*
         I am shifting my operational area to area Madeira and Cape Verde Islands.

On the way south he was reported by a U-boat, whose Commanding Officer did not seem very efficient at recognising men-o'-war.

2307/6/3 *From U.124*
         Two unidentified battleships in position (given).

The Admiral, noting he was in the position signalled, lost no time in telling the U-boat who she was reporting.

On 8th March their luck changed.

0920/8 *From Scharnhorst*
         Convoy in sight (position given).

0930/8 *From Scharnhorst*
         Enemy battleships Malaya class in sight on westerly course.

This time the Admiral advanced more boldly to sound the strength of the escort. Mistaking a destroyer for a cruiser he considered this Sierra Leone convoy was also too tough a proposition.

He therefore reported it, for the benefit of the U-boats, and once again retired with *Scharnhorst*. This is what was seen from the convoy.

1600/8 *From Malaya*
One large vessel, uncertain whether battleship or battle-cruiser (position given) distance 40 miles.

1745/8 *From Malaya*
Enemy in sight. Battlecruiser *Scharnhorst*. My position (given).

1748/8 *From Malaya*
Enemy retiring westward.

Malaya eventually reported the affair as follows:

> *From Malaya to Admiralty*
> During afternoon 8 March *Forester* was sent 10 miles west of convoy to keep down submarines if shadowing. At 1331 she reported ship, apparently warship and was ordered to investigate. At 1410 she reported by W/T sighting top and 1 funnel, and at 1442 possibly *Gneisenau*. *Malaya* and *Faulknor* proceeded clear of convoy to west. *Cecilia* remained with convoy which turned north-east. Further reports showed enemy altering course at high speed. *Malaya* and *Faulknor* continued to close and at 1515 aircraft was catapulted. At 1645 sighted enemy *Scharnhorst* class distance 15 miles. At 1648 enemy altered course to south-west and increased speed. He appeared to have turrets trained fore and aft. Being unable to close range *Malaya* and destroyers turned at once to regain convoy before dark. At 1659 aircraft reported 2 Scharnhorst class, confirmed at 1703. *Malaya* rejoined convoy at 1900. Aircraft lost *Malaya* and force-landed after dark.

In the meantime the U-boats made contact.

0142/9 *From U-124*
Have contacted convoy.

0225/9 *From U-105*
Convoy in sight.

Between them they sank five ships. In the meantime the Admiral was feeling the call of the HX route once more.

2055/9 *From Gneisenau to Gruppe West*
Proceeding to fuel from Erinland. After provisioning proceeding at end of week with supply ships to HX route.

But the German naval staff made reservations.

2100/11 *From German Naval War Staff to Gneisenau*
Operations on HX route permitted only up to 17/3. While still remaining at sea concentrate on causing diversionary action by effective reappearance in Azores and Cape Verde area as soon as possible after 17/3 to facilitate the homeward passage of Hipper and Scheer through Iceland Strait during new moon period. Undue prolongation of current operations not desirable in view of Bismarck and Prinz Eugen being ready for action at end of April and in view of efforts being made to have Gneisenau and Scharnhorst ready for action at the same time. Also possible to divert enemy from passage of Hipper and Scheer through Iceland Straits by a well timed entry into French coast port.

13/3 *From Gneisenau*
Estimate Gneisenau will need 4 weeks and Scharnhorst 10 for repairs.

Again no HX convoy was contacted. Spread out with their auxiliary ships, however, they swept the shipping lanes with the following formidable results.

2157/15 *From Admiralty*
Following intercepted from S.S. *Simnia*. Am being attacked by surface raider in position (given). *Simnia* being shelled.

0308/16 *From Admiralty*
S.S. *Athel Foam* reports being shelled by warship raider in position (given).

0430/16 *From Admiralty*
My 2157/15 and 0308/16. It is possible these attacks were carried out by *Scharnhorst* and *Gneisenau*.

1858/16 *From Admiralty*
S.S. *Metirton* being attacked by surface raider in position (given).

1858/16 *From Admiralty*
S.S. *Demerton* being attacked by surface raider.

2055/16 *From Admiralty*
Following has been intercepted. S.S. *Chilean Reefer* being attacked and shelled by surface raider in position (given).

2129/16 *From Rodney*
One unknown vessel in position (given).

2159/16 *From Rodney*
Enemy almost certainly warship disappeared to north eastward in darkness. One large vessel presumed tanker also seen but lost during darkness. Am rejoining convoy HX 114.

2355/16 *From Rodney*
Captain and Chief Officer of *Chilean Reefer* picked up with 24 survivors, both stating quite clearly enemy warship was *Gneisenau*. Also state she altered course to south eastward after initial retirement to north east. Ship observed by survivors signalling with red and green lights in front bridge to another vessel thought to be tanker referred to.

Once again, a battleship frightened the Germans away, but not before they had accounted for sixteen ships between them. By now Admiral Lutjens knew he had been reported; he believed Force H, consisting of *Renown* and the aircraft carrier *Ark Royal*, was searching for him to the southward. It seemed that the Atlantic was getting a bit hot. So:

0100/19 *From Gneisenau to Gruppe West*
Am returning to Brest.

Gneisenau and *Scharnhorst* anchored at Brest at 0750 on 22nd March, after their greatest combined achievement. In the sixty days they had been at sea together they had steamed 17,800 miles, sinking twenty-two ships totalling 115,622 tons. Admiral Raeder showed his appreciation by means of the following signal:

21st   *From German Naval Commander-in-Chief to Admiral*
March   *Lutjens*

> *On completion of the first occasion in German naval history on which a squadron of our Battleships has operated successfully in the wide spaces of the Atlantic, I congratulate you and your subordinates for the fine resolution you have shown and the splendid results you have achieved. I appreciate the vital part played by supply and escort ships, who also receive my fullest praise. I hope before long to be able to put an even stronger force under your command for a similar operation on the high seas.*

Escape from Brest
12th February 1942

After the *Bismarck* action *Scharnhorst* and *Gneisenau* were joined at Brest by *Prinz Eugen*. During 1941 the three ships were attacked by 1,875 aircraft. 1,962 tons of bombs were hurled at them, and each ship was only hit once. But this could not last. By the beginning of 1942 the ships were obviously doomed if they stayed much longer. At a conference on 12th January Hitler likened them to someone suffering from cancer. Without an operation they would die. An operation might save them.

Against all advice he decided that they should return to Germany by the Channel route. He was convinced the British were incapable of reacting quickly enough to such a bold plan.

The whole operation depended on surprise. It hinged on how far east the ships could get before they were discovered. This meant secrecy in its strictest sense. Apart from secrecy in planning the operations it must be carried out without a whisper. Here are Admiral Cilliax's signed orders for the operation:

"Destroyers are to take into account that changes of course and speed will not be transmitted, as there are no secure means of signalling. THEREFORE VIGILANCE. . . . The compulsory route provided must be sufficient guide for the course to be followed by the formation.

"Wireless is to be used only when there is definite contact with the enemy or if it has first been used by the Officer Commanding the formation or if from an independent observation it is thought that there is acute danger to the formation which can not be averted or indicated by any other means."

Anything involving co-ordinated movement undertaken by people separated from one another is better achieved if it is carried out in silence. The silence suggests those taking part are sure of themselves and their confederates. But this needs practice and more practice. Those concerned must know one another. Here was an operation which demanded this high quality of co-operation but offered little or no practice beforehand, and probably all taking part were strangers.

Nevertheless, by making full use of the gaps between the Royal Air Force bombs, sporadic trials were carried out, and by 4th February the three ships were ready for the fray.

On the morning of 11th February came the signal from Gruppe West to Flag Officer, *Scharnhorst*. It was one of the five code words given to this operation, and it was the warning for the operation to begin that night. Shortly before casting off there was an air raid which delayed the ships getting off the mark.

This was a moment of naval history when a signal of any sort might have brought disaster. Nevertheless one cannot help sympathising with Admiral Cilliax's desire to make a signal at midnight when the formation was 72 minutes astern of schedule. The needle timing planned for contacting his air and surface forces ahead must stand. There was nothing he could do about it except hope that the delay had been observed and checked all the way through. But he always had one consolation. The longer the silence lasted the nearer he was to home.

When 10 o'clock and 10.30 came and went on the following clear morning, there was, to every German's astonishment, NO indication that the formation's presence was known. By 11 the formation had appeared on a British radar screen, 27 miles south-west of Gris Nez, but it had not been taken very seriously. The first sighting, the manner in which they were first reported, is unique and certainly worth a place in this collection.

At the time R.A.F. Fighter Group was engaged in making offensive sweeps, beyond the range of radar, to harass enemy sorties from Northern France. Their long range requirements precluded the planes from carrying wireless or even radio telephone equipment. They were cut off from the world immediately they were airborne. The weather on the morning of the 12th was poor for their job, so the experienced Station Commander, Group Captain Victor Beamish, and Wing Commander Boyd, had taken a hand. They set out on a sweep about 10.00. Off the French coast they sighted two German fighters which they chased at full speed. When they looked down they were amazed to find themselves above two large warships surrounded by escort vessels. Barely had they recognised the ships than they were set upon by a swarm of enemy fighters. They managed to disentangle themselves and streaked for home to report the news by word of mouth at 11.09 as soon as they landed.

The tidings of this alarming affair were, in fact, delivered on foot, as they would have been in the Old Testament.

There was, indeed, a British plan to counter such an operation. The Admiralty had foreseen the likelihood of the enemy breaking eastwards, and had ordered six destroyers and six

MTB's to be at immediate readiness. Vice-Admiral Dover signalled the orders to the destroyers:

> If signal "Proceed in execution of previous orders" is made, destroyers are to proceed forthwith at best speed to NE Hinder Whistle Buoy. You will be kept informed of movements of enemy ships through Dover Strait, and you should endeavour to intercept in the approximate (position given). Motor Torpedo Boats will not operate north of (latitude given). Acknowledge.

On the fateful night of 11th/12th February this precaution had been signalled to the destroyers.

2017/11 *From Vice Admiral Dover to Captain of 21st Destroyer*
Feb./42 *Flotilla*
> Come to 15 minutes notice at 0400/12 and revert to 4 hours notice at 0700/12 unless otherwise ordered.

But to be effective, any plan of attack by us needed more time to develop than was given by an announcement that the enemy was passing Le Touquet at high speed. At 11.45 Vice Admiral Dover directed his only available cat towards the pigeons.

1145 *From Vice Admiral Dover to Destroyers*
> Proceed in execution of previous orders.

At 12.22 the Motor Torpedo Boats attacked, at 1245 torpedo carrying aircraft attacked, around 1600 the Destroyers attacked. *Scharnhorst* struck two mines, *Gneisenau* one. Admiral Cilliax transferred to a destroyer, it broke down. The formation became separated. But all three ships arrived in German ports, afloat, and the following day brought this signal:

1420/ *From German Naval Commander-in-Chief to Admiral*
13 Feb. *Cilliax*
> *The transfer of the Brest Group into the German Bight, having been carefully planned by Staffs and Escort groups, was carried out with exemplary dash and skill. I convey to you, your commanding officers, your officers and crews my*

*congratulations in recognition of this operation. I have asked
the Commander-in-Chief Air to convey my thanks to all
those who took part.*

The Sinking of SCHARNHORST
26th December 1943

On Christmas Day, 1943, *Scharnhorst* lay anchored up a fjord on
the north coast of Norway. The damaged *Tirpitz* lay there too,
but no *Gneisenau*. After all the adventures they had been through
together their partnership had ended. Down south *Gneisenau*
burned for three days after R.A.F. bombers had pounded her in
a German dockyard. Her fighting days were over.

It was sad, but it had no effect on the morale of *Scharnhorst*.
She was a proud ship. She had a ship's company who believed in
her. At that particular moment they also believed they were set
for an enjoyable and relaxed Christmas.

The Christmas mail had been distributed, Captain's rounds
were over. They had been quite informal. So far the men liked
Captain Hintz, but he had only taken over command in October
and had not yet taken the ship to sea. Before him had been
Captain Hueffmeier. It was not difficult to be an improvement on
him. He was unpopular and worse still, he was no seaman. He
had put the ship ashore, he had collided with a U-boat. Why on
earth did they ever have to promote his predecessor, Captain
Hoffman, to Admiral? Captain Hoffman was worshipped by
everyone. He was the man who had built up their morale and
made the ship unsinkable. So much for her Captains. There lay
the ship, peaceful and majestic in a setting appropriate for a
Christmas card.

And it was peaceful, at least it was up to 1 p.m. Then, through
the ship's loudspeakers, came the jarring warning to prepare for
sea. Throughout the afternoon came other tiresome and disturb-
ing messages. At five, Rear Admiral Bey and his staff bundled

on board from *Tirpitz*, for their own Admiral Kummetz was on leave. At seven *Scharnhorst* slid through the Arctic gloom down the fjord accompanied by five destroyers.

Ahead of them, up in the Barents Strait steamed their objective, a Russian-bound convoy. This had just been made clear in a signal from Admiral Doenitz.

> *From German Commander-in-Chief to Scharnhorst*
> *Attack and destroy the convoy to alleviate the struggle of your comrades on the Eastern front.*

Escorting the convoy were fifteen destroyers and two corvettes, led by the captain of the 17th Destroyer Flotilla in *Onslow*. Supporting the escort were the cruisers *Sheffield*, *Norfolk* and their flagship *Belfast*. In the background lay the Commander-in-Chief, Home Fleet in *Duke of York*, with the cruiser *Jamaica*, and four destroyers.

In latitudes where no daylight relieves the night at that time of year, and in brutal, raw weather, the situation on Boxing Day, 1943, developed thus:

0652 *From C.-in-C. to Belfast*
   Close convoy for mutual support.

When the crew of *Scharnhorst* went to Action Stations at 0700 she was struggling into the teeth of an Arctic gale. The peace of the anchorage they had left had faded completely.

0720 *From Scharnhorst to Destroyers*
   Seek and shadow convoy.

0825 *From Z29 (destroyer leader)*
   Silhouette sighted distance 4 miles.

The German destroyer crews were new and inexperienced and probably very seasick. Most of the signals which passed between them and *Scharnhorst* were too garbled to be intercepted and recorded. Nevertheless inexperience alone hardly explains why the German flotilla took such a small part in the action which follows.

0844 *From Belfast*
   Unidentified Radar contact on bearing 295°, 16 miles.

0906 *From Sheffield*
Unidentified Radar contact on bearing 258°, 10 miles.

0906 *From Norfolk*
Unidentified Radar contact on bearing 261°, 12 miles.

0922 *From Belfast*
Enemy in sight bearing 222°.
(Cruisers passed reports of enemy continuously until 1044.)

0927 *From Belfast to Norfolk*
Open fire.
(About 0930 a shell, probably from *Norfolk*, disabled Scharnhorst's Radar equipment which, in this low visibility, virtually "blinded" her.)

0946 *From Belfast*
Enemy's speed 28 knots.

0955 *From Scharnhorst*
Have been fired on in (position given) by what appeared to be a cruiser using radar-controlled firing apparatus.

0958 *From C.-in-C. to Onslow (repeated Belfast)*
Send 4 destroyers to join *Belfast*.

1001 *From Scharnhorst*
Check fire.

1012 *From Scharnhorst*
Aircraft reported unidentified vessel in (position given) thought to be Commander-in-Chief, Home Fleet.

1013 *From Z29*
Am advancing into immediate vicinity of convoy, according to plan. Course 230°, speed 12 knots.

1020 *From Onslow to C.-in-C. (repeated Belfast)*
Musketeer, Matchless, Opportune, Virago detailed.

1044 *From Belfast*
Have lost touch with enemy who is steering north. Am closing convoy.
(By steering north at high speed, *Scharnhorst* hoped to work round behind the cruisers and attack the convoy.)

1055 *From Scharnhorst to Destroyers*
What is your position, course and speed.

1103 *From C.-in-C. to Belfast*
Unless touch can be regained by some unit there is no chance of my finding enemy.

1125 *From C.-in-C. to Onslow*
Use your discretion regarding mean course of convoy.

1131 *From Onslaught (with convoy) to Onslow*
Have obtained Radar contact bearing 150°, 6½ miles.

1134 *From Onslow to Onslaught*
Investigate.

1135 *From Belfast*
Onslaught's contact is me.

1205 *From Belfast*
Unidentified Radar contact bearing 075°, 13 miles.

1220 *From Belfast*
Enemy in sight bearing 090°.

1220 *From Belfast to Cruisers*
Open fire.

1230 *From Norfolk to Belfast*
Norfolk hit aft.

1240 *From Scharnhorst*
Scharnhorst in action with several units in position (given) and being fired on by one heavy unit using radar-controlled firing apparatus.

In this encounter *Sheffield* had a near miss from *Scharnhorst*. She reported later that bits of shell up to football size came inboard.

1253 *From C.-in-C.*
Enemy aircraft is shadowing me.

1256 *From Gruppe-North*
All aircraft withdrawn on account of weather

1318 *From C.-in-C. to Belfast*
Report composition of enemy.

1325 *From Belfast*
One heavy ship.

1418 *From Scharnhorst to Destroyers*
Break away, put into harbour.

1435 *From C.-in-C. to Belfast*
Have you destroyers in company.

1442 *From Belfast*
No, they are following.

1449 *From C.-in-C.*
If practicable, intend to engage from the westward on a similar course.

1450 *From Belfast*
Enemy position course and speed (given).

1551 *From C.-in-C. to Home Fleet in Company*
The estimated bearing and distance of the enemy from me are 025°, 25 miles.

1551 *From Norfolk*
I have a fire in my wing compartment oil fuel tank. Cannot be controlled unless ship stops rolling.

1612 *From Belfast to Sheffield*
Come on.

1620 *From Sheffield to Belfast*
Am following you. My maximum speed is 23 knots.

1635 *From C.-in-C. to Belfast*
Prepare to fire star-shell over enemy.

1636 *From C.-in-C.*
Unidentified Radar contact on bearing 020°, 13 miles.

1640 *From C.-in-C. to Destroyers in Company*
Take up advantageous positions for firing torpedoes but do not attack until ordered.

   (At 1645 *Duke of York* opened fire, by Radar, on *Scharnhorst*.)

1646 *From C.-in-C. to Belfast*
Open fire with star-shell.

After the second engagement with the cruisers *Scharnhorst* seemed to abandon the idea of attacking the convoy. The crew relaxed. Some were allowed to leave their Action Stations where they had been for nine cold hours. Except for the Radar the ship was undamaged. With their speed, and nothing opposing them heavier than cruisers they could withdraw when they chose. The heavy gun flashes of *Duke of York* followed by the arrival of armour-piercing shell was therefore a very unpleasant surprise.

1656 *From Scharnhorst*
      Am in action with heavy Battleship.

1657 *From Scharnhorst*
      My position (given) maintaining contact.

1700 *From Admiral, Norway*
      U-boats form a new patrol line (given).

1702 *From C.-in-C. to Belfast*
      Any further news.

1713 *From C.-in-C. to Destroyers in Company*
      Destroyers close and attack with torpedoes as soon as possible.

1720 *From Belfast*
      Out of touch.

1723 *From C.-in-C. to Belfast*
      Steer south to get between enemy and his base.

1724 *From Scharnhorst*
      Am surrounded by a strong force.

1724 *From C.-in-C. to Belfast*
      Steer 140° and join me.

1808 *From C.-in-C.*
      By Radar enemy bears 070°, 9 miles.

1811 *From C.-in-C. to Scorpion* (destroyer)
      Can you report my fall of shot.

1813 *From Scorpion*
      Your last salvo 200 yards short.

1815 *From Admiral, Norway*
      U-boats close Scharnhorst at full speed.

1816 *From Scorpion*
      Can only see occasional splashes owing to smoke.
      (After 52nd salvo, about this time, *Duke of York* checked fire to allow destroyers to press home torpedo attacks.)

1828 *From C.-in-C.*
By Radar enemy bears 069°, 10 miles.

1847 *From C.-in-C. to Belfast*
I see little hope of catching *Scharnhorst* and am proceeding
to support convoy.

At 1830 *Scharnhorst's* speed was still undiminished and she was
drawing out of range of *Duke of York*, still confident of escape.
Then grey shadows emerged which turned into British destroyers.
At this stage there was an argument between the 1st and 2nd
Gunnery Control Officer on account of which the vital secondary
armament barrage was delayed. This allowed our destroyers to
creep relentlessly into their attacking positions.

1852 *From Savage* (destroyer)
Am proceeding to attack.

1852 *From Scorpion*
Attack completed.

1853 *From Stord* (destroyer)
Attack completed.

1853 *From Savage*
Attack completed.
(There were several underwater explosions heard in
Belfast at 1858.)

1900 *From Scharnhorst to The Fuehrer*
We shall fight to the last shell. Scharnhorst onwards.

In a Broadcast from the bridge Captain Hintz said to ship's
company:
I shake you all by the hand for the last time.

1906 *From C.-in-C. to Jamaica*
Finish her off with torpedoes.

1944 *From C.-in-C.*
All destroyers without torpedoes join me.

1954 *From C.-in-C. to Home Fleet in Company*
Clear the area of the target except for those ships with
torpedoes and one destroyer with searchlight.

1956 *From Scorpion*
      A lot of wreckage on sea, am closing now.

2012 *From Scorpion*
      Am picking up German survivors.

2015 *From C.-in-C.*
      Please confirm *Scharnhorst* is sunk.

2018 *From Scorpion*
      Survivors are from *Scharnhorst.*

(It was a coincidence that the Captain of the destroyer *Scorpion* bore a strong physical resemblance to the German Admiral Bey. This was almost too much for the German survivors.)

2019 *From C.-in-C.*
      Has *Scharnhorst* sunk.

2032 *From Belfast*
      Satisfied that *Scharnhorst* is sunk. Where shall I join you.

2100 *From C.-in-C. to Admiralty*
      Scharnhorst sunk.

2153 *From Admiralty to C.-in-C. (repeated Belfast)*
      Grand. Well done.

SCHARNHORST

GNEISENAU

POSTHUMOUS V.C.

On 9th April, 1940, information indicated that Narvik—the important railhead and harbour of the Norwegian Iron Ore industry—was only lightly held by the enemy. They would not, we thought, have had time to consolidate themselves after their northern drive through Norway. The Second Destroyer Flotilla consisting of *Hardy* (Captain B. A. Warburton-Lee), *Havock*, *Hunter*, *Hotspur* and *Hostile* were detached to attack the harbour.

On the way Captain Warburton-Lee gathered from Norwegians that our intelligence underestimated the true facts. Not that this deterred him as may be seen from this signal.

1751/9   *From Captain Warburton-Lee to Admiralty*
April   Norwegians report Germans holding Narvik in force, six destroyers and one submarine, channel is possibly mined. Intend attacking at dawn high water.

The Admiralty replied:

0136/10   *From Admiralty*
           Norwegian coast defence ships *Eidsvold* and *Norge* may be in German hands. You alone can judge whether in these circumstances attack should be made. We shall support whatever decision you take.

Captain Warburton-Lee drew up his plan of attack and passed it by signal through the snowstorms to his flotilla, as follows:

Following orders for operation T.N. Final approach to Narvik *Hardy* will close Pilot Station which is close to Steinhos Light. *Hunter* will follow in support. *Hotspur* and *Havock* are to provide anti-submarine protection to the northward. Ships are to be at Action Stations from 0030. When passing Skredneset Light *Hardy* will pass close to shore and order a line of bearing. Thereafter ships are to maintain narrow quarterline to starboard so that fire from all ships is effective ahead. On closing Narvik *Hardy* will

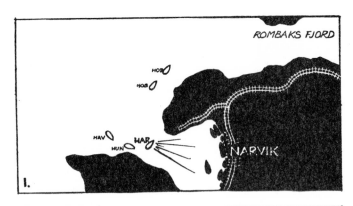

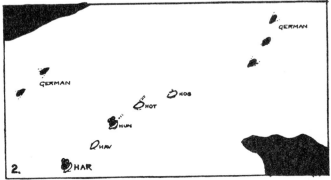

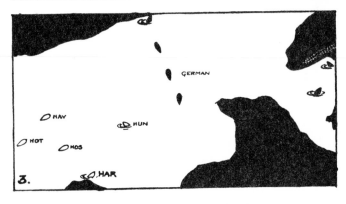

steer for inner harbour with *Hunter* astern in support. . . .
Germans may have several destroyers and a submarine in
vicinity. Some probably on patrol. Ships are to engage all
targets immediately and keep a particular lookout for enemy
who may be berthed in inlets. On approaching Narvik
Hardy, *Hunter*, *Havock* engage enemy ships inside harbour
with guns and torpedoes. *Hotspur* engage ships to North
West. *Hostile* assist on either target. Prepare to lay
smoke for cover and to tow disabled ships. If opposition is
silenced landing parties (less *Hotspur*) when ordered to land
make for Ore Quay unless otherwise ordered. *Hardy's*
first lieutenant in charge. Additional visual signal to withdraw will be one Red and one Green Very light from *Hardy*.
Half outfit of torpedoes is to be fired unless target warrants
more. In order to relieve congestion of movements all ships
when turning to fire or opening are to keep turning to port
if possible. Watch adjacent ships. Keep moderate speed.

At 0415 *Hardy*, *Hunter* and *Havock* entered Narvik harbour.
The attack was a complete surprise. At 0515 the attack was
repeated. By this time visibility was clearing and opposition from
shore batteries and ships was increasing. At 0551 three enemy
destroyers were seen approaching from the north-east. Captain
Warburton-Lee, having done all the damage he could, ordered
his ships to withdraw. No sooner had the flotilla formed on a
westerly course than they ran into two more German destroyers
approaching from ahead.

Hardy, burning, beached herself to the southward. Her Captain
was killed. *Hunter* was sunk. The last signal from *Hardy* was
made at 0555:

KEEP ON ENGAGING THE ENEMY

Hotspur who had been damaged in collision with *Hunter*,
managed to withdraw to the south-westward, covered by *Hostile*
and *Havock*. The enemy losses were as follows: Destroyers
Heidkamp, *Schmitt*, sunk. *Arnim*, *Roeder*, *Kumme*, *Thiele*, damaged.
Seven or eight merchant ships were sunk. Captain Bernard
Warburton-Lee was awarded a posthumous Victoria Cross.

"ONE ENEMY BATTLESHIP"
1941

22nd May

1619 *From Admiralty*
Photographs show *Bismarck* Class battleship in Bergen with cargo type merchant ships in vicinity. *Hipper* Class Cruiser nearby and destroyer with three cargo type merchant ships and six auxiliaries, apparently minesweepers, in the vicinity. Destroyer has oiler alongside. One merchant ship berthing alongside *Hipper* Class cruiser.

1939 *From Hatson Air Station*
Following received from Hatson reconnaissance aircraft over Bergen. Battleship and cruiser have left.

1942 *From Commander-in-Chief Home Fleet. H.M.S. King George V (hereafter C.-in-C.)*
Prepare for sea.

2042 *C.-in-C. to Arethusa, Manchester.*
Arethusa is to proceed to take up patrol line. *Manchester* on arrival in area is to take *Birmingham* and *Arethusa* under his orders and dispose ships to patrol the Iceland-Faroes passage to westward of mine barrier.

2043 *From C.-in-C.*
Request Air reconnaissance be maintained as follows:—
(a) Iceland-Faroes channel.
(b) Denmark Strait.
(c) Faroes-Shetland channel.
(d) Norwegian Coast.

Object to detect enemy battleship and cruiser breaking out to westward. Request all forces and authorities be informed of patrols instituted.

2045 *From C.-in-C.*

Intend to proceed in *King George V* with *Victorious, Galatea, Hermione, Kenya, Aurora,* and seven destroyers passing through Hoxa boom at 2300 Thursday 22 May (initial route given). Commander-in-Chief Rosyth is requested to arrange anti-submarine air escort from daylight 23 May. Code word REBEL.

Repulse is to join me by noon 23 May.

In the absence of other information intend Rear-Admiral Commanding Second Cruiser Squadron (hereafter *Galatea*) in *Galatea* with *Hermione* to patrol to westward off N. Rona-Faroes minefield.

2101 *From Admiralty*

Positions of our submarines at 0800/23 and movements the following 24 hours include P.31 from patrol position proceeding to patrol 25 miles west of Stadlandet. May be proceeding on surface.

2210 *From Admiral, Iceland*

Sailed *Arethusa.*

2212 *From Admiral, Iceland*

Sailed *Suffolk.*

23rd May

0630 *From Admiral, Rosyth*

Air reconnaissance postponed owing to weather.

1009 *From Rear-Admiral Commanding First Cruiser Squadron in Norfolk (hereafter Norfolk)*

Suffolk is to patrol within RDF distance of ice edge on a line running North-East and South-West. When clear inshore *Norfolk* will patrol about 15 miles abeam of you. When thick inshore, *Norfolk* will patrol to cover inshore passage. *Norfolk* will make contact with you at 1300 on 24 May. Investigate ice up to minefield on parting company today Friday.

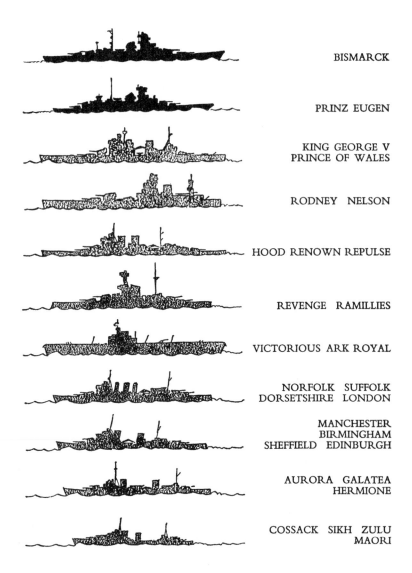

BISMARCK

PRINZ EUGEN

KING GEORGE V
PRINCE OF WALES

RODNEY   NELSON

HOOD RENOWN REPULSE

REVENGE   RAMILLIES

VICTORIOUS ARK ROYAL

NORFOLK   SUFFOLK
DORSETSHIRE   LONDON

MANCHESTER
BIRMINGHAM
SHEFFIELD   EDINBURGH

AURORA   GALATEA
HERMIONE

COSSACK   SIKH   ZULU
MAORI

1017 *From Norfolk to Suffolk*
Enemy may be expected to separate in low visibility or while heavy ship holds off our forces. Intend that *Norfolk* shall try to keep visual contact and engage cruiser if she leaves *Bismarck*. *Suffolk's* object is to shadow *Bismarck*.

1817 *From Admiral, Iceland*
Study of recent air reconnaisances shows that a well-built ship could make a passage through Denmark Strait about 50 miles inside ice edge.

1922 *From Suffolk to Norfolk*
One battleship, one cruiser in sight bearing 020 degrees distant 7 miles. Course 240 degrees. (*Suffolk's* position given.)

1939 *From Vice Admiral Commanding Battle Cruisers in Hood (hereafter Hood)*
Raise steam for full speed.

2032 *From Norfolk*
One battleship, one cruiser in sight (position 2 on diagram).

Note. Norfolk and Suffolk then continued to shadow *Bismarck* and pass reports continually. *Suffolk* made thirty reports by Signal from 1922/23 until 0538/24.

2055 *From Hood to escorting Destroyers*
If you are unable to maintain this speed I will have to go on without you. You should follow at your best speed.

2114 *From C.-in-C. to Galatea*
Take *Kenya, Hermione* and endeavour to locate enemy.

2137 *From Admiral, Iceland to Malcolm*
Proceed when ready to locate enemy reported in (position 2)

2253 *Admiralty to Vice Admiral Commanding Force H in Renown at Gibraltar (hereafter Force H)*
Raise steam for full speed.

2256 *From C.-in-C. to Galatea*
I am hoping *Hood* may head them off and force them to turn back or to the Southward. Maintain present bearing 7 miles.

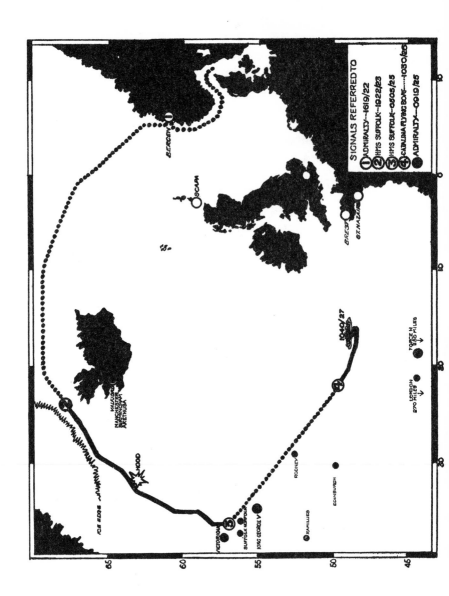

SIGNALS REFERRED TO

① ADMIRALTY—1619/22
② H.M.S. SUFFOLK—1922/23
③ H.M.S. SUFFOLK—0605/25
④ CATALINA FLYING BOAT—1030/25
⑤ ADMIRALTY—0919/25

2308 *From C.-in-C. to Victorious*
Primary tasks which will be required of *Victorious* aircraft
are Reconnaissance and Shadowing, bearing in mind that
the enemy may divide his force. A Secondary task may be
provision of torpedo striking force.
If enemy is engaged, *Victorious* with *Aurora* and two rear
destroyers from each wing of Screen is to break off to
disengaged side.

24th May

0050 *From Admiralty to Force H*
Proceed as soon as ready to join (convoy) after daylight
May 26th. Should reconnaissance today indicate one or both
German Battle Cruisers have left Brest it will be necessary
to alter these instructions.

0120 *From Admiralty*
If still complying with C.-in-CHF's instructions and in
absence of other orders from him, *Manchester, Birmingham,
Arethusa, Galatea, Hermione* should rendezvous 30 miles East
of Langanaes to form a patrol line in event of enemy
breaking back.

0537 *From Prince of Wales*
(Enemy sighting report) distant 17 miles.

0544 *From Hood*
(Enemy sighting report) distant 14 miles.

0552 *From Bismarck*
Am engaging two heavy units.

0615 *From Norfolk*
Hood blown up in position (given).

0624 *From Prince of Wales to Norfolk*
Hood is sunk. My bridge is out of action. Y turret out of
action temporarily. Otherwise damage appears superficial.
Will confirm.

0628 *From Norfolk to Prince of Wales*
I intend to keep in touch with the enemy.

0632 *From Bismarck*
Battlecruiser, probably Hood, sunk. Another battleship King George or Renown damaged and turned off. Two heavy cruisers maintaining contact.

(Note: *Prince of Wales* was mistaken for *King George V* throughout)

0637 *Norfolk to Destroyers in company*
Hood sunk in position (given) proceed to search for survivors.

0705 *From Bismarck*
Have sunk a battleship in approximate position (given).

0720 *From Prince of Wales*
A and B turrets in action. Y turret two guns in action. About 400 tons of water in ship mainly abaft armoured bulkhead. Compartment above steering compartment flooded but steering gear in action. Estimated best speed 27 knots.

0731 *Norfolk to Prince of Wales*
Open out to 10 miles. I may have to fall back on you if the Cruiser tries to drive me off.

0801 *From Bismarck*
   1. Electrical engine-room No. 4 broken down.
   2. Port boiler-room No. 2 is making water but can be held. Water in forecastle.
   3. Maximum speed 28 knots.
   4. Two enemy radar sets recognised.
   5. Intention to put into St. Nazaire. No losses of personnel.

0839 *From Admiralty to Manchester, Birmingham, Arethusa*
Proceed with all dispatch.

0903 *From Admiralty to Rodney*
Proceed with *Britannic* and Screen at best speed, course 290°.

0906 *From Electra*
Intend landing the three survivors from *Hood* at Reykjavik.

0943 *From Admiral, Iceland to Malcolm*
Sunderland (flying boat) reports survivors in position (given).

1007 *From Prince of Wales*
Main armament control undamaged. 9 main armament guns in action. Secondary armament guns in action. Considerable damage bridge. Both forward High Angle Directors out of action. About 600 tons of water in ship, mainly aft, from two or more hits about water line. Estimate maximum speed 26 knots.

1036 *From Admiralty to Rodney*
If *Britannic* cannot keep up, leave her behind with 1 destroyer.

1110 *From Admiralty to Revenge (Halifax)*
Revenge is to raise steam with all despatch and proceed to sea.

1126 *From Admiralty to Norfolk*
Continue shadowing *Bismarck* even if you run out of fuel in order that C.-in-C. may catch up in time.

1144 *From Admiralty to Ramillies*
Proceed so as to make contact with enemy from westwards, subsequently placing enemy between *Ramillies* and C.-in-C.

1206 *From Admiralty to Galatea*
Unless otherwise ordered by C.-in-C., *Galatea* and *Hermione* are to proceed to Faroes and fuel.

1210 *From Norfolk*
Visibility decreasing.

1235 *From Admiral, Iceland*
Plot of Sunderland flying boat on return appears to indicate *Norfolk's* position accurate. *Bismarck* leaving considerable wake of oil fuel.

1238 *From Admiralty*
Situation at 1100.

Bismarck and *Prinz Eugen* in position (given) course 215°, speed 24 knots. *Bismarck* has received some damage.
(2) C.S.1. in *Norfolk* with *Prince of Wales* and *Suffolk* are in touch with enemy. *Prince of Wales* has 2 guns out of action. *Hood* blown up by unlucky hit. C.-in-C. in *King George V*

with *Repulse, Victorious, Kenya, Aurora* may be about 230 miles to eastward of enemy's position.

(3) *Rodney* in position (given) with 3 or 4 destroyers has been ordered to steer best closing course.

(4) *Ramillies* in position (given) has been ordered to place herself to westward of enemy.

(5) *Manchester* is taking *Birmingham* and *Arethusa* under his orders and establishing patrol line north of Langanaes, North East of Iceland.

(6) C.S.2. in *Galatea* with *Hermione* is being ordered to fuel at Faroes.

(7) Force H left Gibraltar at 0200/24 and is proceeding westwards.

(8) *Revenge* is about to leave Halifax with orders to close enemy.

(9) *Edinburgh* in approximate position (given) is being ordered to close and take over Stand-by Shadower.

(10) Enemy battle cruisers were in Brest yesterday 23/May.

1250 *From Admiralty to Edinburgh*
Close enemy last reported position (given) so as to take over Stand-by Shadower if necessary. Fuel should be conserved reasonably while closing and speed of 25 knots is suggested, but after contact *NO* consideration of fuel must allow you to lose contact.

1314 *From Norfolk*
Have lost touch with enemy in low visibility.

1314 *From C.-in-C. to Repulse*
If this course and speed is continued, report when you must leave to return to Hvalfjord at 20 knots.

1340 *Repulse to C.-in-C.*
At 0500 tomorrow Sunday. This will get me back to Hvalfjord with 8·5% useable fuel remaining.

1349 *Norfolk*
One battleship one cruiser in sight (position given).

1348 *From Bismarck*
1400 approximate position (given) King George with cruiser is

maintaining contact. Intention: If no engagement intend to shake off enemy during night.

1350 *From 1st Sea Lord to Chief of Naval Staff, Canada*
Reference Admiralty's appreciation of general situation, I shall be grateful if you would hold long distance aircraft available for reconnaissance from Newfoundland.

1355 *Galatea to C.-in-C.*
I hope they won't get nervous when we don't turn up.

1417 *C.-in-C. to Galatea*
Admiralty is being informed that you are in company.

1420 *From Bismarck to Prinz Eugen*
Intend to shake off enemy as follows. During rain showers Bismarck will move off on westerly course. Prinz Eugen to maintain course and speed until she is forced to alter course or 3 hours after leaving Bismarck. Following this she is to oil from Belchen or Lothringen and afterwards to engage in cruiser warfare independently. Executive on Code word HOOD.

1440 *From C.-in-C. to Galatea*
Take *Victorious* and cruisers to provide a screen for her under your orders and steer for nearest position within 100 miles of *Bismarck* and from there launch torpedo bomber attacks. *Victorious* is not to come under gunfire from enemy ships. As cruisers run short of fuel they are to be detached to Reykjavik. *Victorious* is to maintain contact as long as torpedo bomber or reconnaissance aircraft are available. *King George V* is altering course more to the Southward.

1442 *From Bismarck to U-boats*
West boats collect in approximate position (given) at dawn. Am approaching from North. Intend to draw heavy units shadowing Bismarck through this area.

1445 *From Admiralty to Norfolk*
Report as follows regarding *Bismarck*:
(1) Percentage of fighting efficiency remaining.
(2) Ammunition expended.
(3) Reasons for frequent alteration of course.

Request your intentions as regards *Prince of Wales* re-engaging. Keep a good look-out for U-boats.

1504 *From German Western Naval Headquarters, Paris (hereafter called Group West) to Bismarck*
English unit made tactical signal at 1223 from approximate position (given). Aircraft reports sighted 12 merchant ships 4 destroyers (position given approximately).

1508 *From Bismarck*
Hood annihilated within 5 minutes by gunfire this morning at 0600. King George turned off after being hit. Bismarck's speed limited. Slightly down by bows owing to hit forward.

1511 *From Group West to Bismarck*
Air reconnaissance of Scapa started. English unit made following to Scapa at 1329. One enemy battleship one cruiser (position given). Renown, Ark Royal and Sheffield left Gibraltar on unknown course during night of 23/24.

1532 *Norfolk to Flying Boat*
Can you report bearing and distance of *Suffolk* on starboard quarter of enemy. Please tell her bearing and distance of enemy.

1535 *From Flying Boat to Norfolk*
Suffolk bears 262 degrees 26 miles, course 140 degrees. She knows enemy position.

1540 *Norfolk to Flying Boat*
Are enemy ships together.

1541 *Flying Boat to Norfolk*
Ships 2 miles apart.

1619 *Norfolk to Admiralty*
Reply to your 1445/24
(1) Uncertain but high.
(2) Engagement 20 minutes also some rounds at cruisers. About 150 expended.
(3) Unaccountable except as effort to shake us off.
Consider *Prince of Wales* should not re-engage until other heavy ships are in contact, unless interception fails. Doubtful if she has speed to force action.

1711 *From Group West to Bismarck*
U-boats will be in approximate position (given) tomorrow morning.

1715 *Norfolk to Prince of Wales*
As in this visibility we are likely to meet the enemy inside gun range, I am putting you ahead.

1738 *Repulse to C.-in-C.*
If you continue on present course and speed until noon tomorrow I find I can remain with you providing that I then proceed to Conception Bay, Newfoundland at economical speed, arriving with 5% useable fuel.

1747 *C.-in-C. to Repulse*
I am afraid your lack of fuel would not enable you to make contact. Intend detaching you to Reykjavik with destroyers at 2100. Destroyers should have fuel for speed of 20 knots.

1756 *Admiralty to London*
Part company with *Arundel Castle* and destroyers. Order them to proceed in execution of previous orders. *London* proceed at economical speed towards position (given). Your movements should be adjusted to close enemy and you should prepare to take over shadowing duties.

1842 *From Group West to Bismarck*
Hearty congratulations.
Preparations being made at St. Nazaire and Brest concur with intentions of Prinz Eugen. If possible to shake off enemy withdrawal to remote sea area seems advisable for Bismarck. Assume Bismarck's maximum speed 28 knots. Report when draught is above normal.

1914 *From Bismarck*
Short engagement with King George without result. Detached Prinz Eugen to oil. Enemy maintains contact.

1916 *Admiralty to Norfolk, Suffolk*
Shadowing by *Norfolk* and *Suffolk* has been admirable. Keep it up and good luck.

1925 *From Group West to Bismarck*
5 U-boats will form patrol line at 0600 between (positions given).

One U-boat in (position given) One U-boat in (position given).
Attacks only against enemy warships.
Air reconnaissance Scapa today shows 3 battleships.
Dummies are possible.

1926 *Norfolk to Prince of Wales*
Do not open fire except in response as I do not want to force the enemy away to the westward.

1934 *Norfolk to C.-in-C.*
Enemy turned away when engaged at long range at 1832. Engagement was broken off to avoid forcing him further away from you. Am shadowing him from 232° distance 18 miles.

2010 *Admiralty*
Unless other orders have been received from C.-in-C., *Manchester, Birmingham* and *Arethusa* are *NOT* to establish patrol ordered by Admiralty but are to proceed to Hvalfjord and fuel.

2012 *Admiralty*
U.S.A. patrol squadron No. 52 (Catalinas) from Argentia, Newfoundland, has been directed to search area 500 miles SE of Cape Farewell.

2030 *Admiralty*
Oiler *Cairndale* fitted for oiling at sea and with scuttling charges has been sailed from Gibraltar to patrol (position given). *Severn* (submarine) will escort *Cairndale* who is expected to reach patrol area about 31 May.

Oiler is being sent to St. John's, Newfoundland. Capital ships can be fuelled in emergency from oiler in Conception Bay. There are tankers in convoys HX127 and 128 with fuel oil. Enquiries are being made whether any U.S. oiler facilities can be made available.

Oiler *San Adolfo* has been ordered to patrol in (position given) which she should reach about 28 May.

2056 *From Bismarck*
Impossible to shake off enemy owing to Radar. Proceeding directly to Brest owing to fuel situation.

2102 *From Galatea to Victorious*
If enemy situation remains the same, alter course and fly off
air striking force at 2200. After flying off intend to steer
220° maintaining 28 knots.

2106 *From Norfolk*
Enemy speed appears to be 22 knots now. Enemy cruiser is
probably to the westward of enemy battleship. *Prince of
Wales* close astern of me. *Suffolk* on my starboard beam.

2138 *Admiralty to Force H*
In case your force is required for extended operations,
destroyers should be sent back to Gibraltar before it is
necessary to give them any fuel.

2144 *Norfolk to Suffolk*
I congratulate you on your very fine shadowing. We may
rely on you again tonight.

2156 *C.-in-C.*
Hope to engage from the Eastward about 0900/25.

2205 *From Suffolk to Norfolk*
I can still see *Bismarck* and think I can see cruiser to the
westward of her.

2211 *From Group West to Bismarck*
*In Scapa not 3 battleships and 3 cruisers as previously reported
but only two probably light cruisers and gunnery training ships.
In the opinion of the Group the enemy is Prince of Wales.*

2217 *Suffolk*
Battleship altering course and firing A.A.

2314 *From Group West to Bismarck*
*Assume it is no longer intended to proceed to position (given) but
to go direct to St. Nazaire.*
Make proposals for deployment of 5 U-boats.
Assume earliest time of arrival is evening of 26th.

2315 *Suffolk to Norfolk*
Aircraft approaching from 124°.

2331 *Admiralty to Force H*
Steer so as to intercept *Bismarck* from Southward. Enemy

must be short of fuel and will have to make for an oiler. Her future movements may guide you to this oiler.

2338 *From Bismarck*
Air attack in approximate position (given).

2351 *Victorious aircraft to Norfolk*
Interrogative O.K.

2352 *Norfolk to Victorious aircraft*
O.K.

25th May

0001 *Victorious aircraft to Victorious*
Have attacked enemy with torpedoes. One hit only observed.

0010 *From Norfolk to Prince of Wales*
One enemy battleship in sight bearing 211°. Open fire.

0020 *Prince of Wales to Norfolk*
I am not certain that was *Bismarck*.

0028 *From Bismarck*
Attack by carrier borne aircraft. Torpedo hit starboard.

0037 *From Bismarck*
Further attacks expected.

0106 *From Suffolk*
Consider enemy speed under 20 knots.

0129 *From Group West to Bismarck*
Unit, probably Admiral in King George class battleship repeatedly made three figure tactical Signals. Last shadowing report was received at 2234.
Discovery of enemy Radar frequency will be useful for fitting jamming gear later.

0153 *From Bismarck*
Torpedo hit of no importance.

0252 *From Group West to Bismarck*
Afternoon 25th intend to carry out air reconnaissance with FW.200 in area North Spanish coast, Brest, Southern tip of Ireland and as far as possible to the west.
6 U-boats will form a patrol line between (position given).

0401 *From Bismarck*
Enemy radar gear with a range of at least 35,000 metres interferes with operations in Atlantic to considerable extent. In Denmark Strait ships were located and enemy maintained contact. Not possible to shake off enemy despite most favourable weather conditions. Will be unable to oil unless succeed in shaking off enemy by superior speed. Running engagement at range of 28,000 metres to 18,000 metres. Hood concentrated fire on Bismarck. Hood destroyed through explosion after 5 minutes. After that target shifted to King George which turned off making black smoke after she received some hits and remained out of sight for several hours. Own expenditure of ammunition 93 rounds. After this King George continued action at maximum range. Bismarck received 2 hits from King George which reduced the speed and put oil bunkers out of action. Prinz Eugen succeeded in escaping because Bismarck engaged cruisers and battleship in fog. Own radar gear liable to break down especially when guns are firing.

0505 *Suffolk to Norfolk*
Lost touch with enemy at 0306 (position 3 on diagram).

0552 *Norfolk to C.-in-C.*
Request air search at dawn. Enemy's speed has not exceeded 22 knots for some time.

0605 *Norfolk to C.-in-C.*
Enemy lost at 0306. *Suffolk* is being sent to search to westward. At daylight *Norfolk* follows *Suffolk* and *Prince of Wales* will be sent to join you.

0840 *From Force H*
My position and course (given) speed 22 knots. *Ark Royal* and *Sheffield* in company. Destroyers detached.

0846 *From Group West to Bismarck*
Last enemy contact report 0213. After that 3 figure tactical reports but no more position reports. We have impression that contact has been lost. Operational signals are repeated to Bermuda and Halifax but not to Gibraltar or Force H which is supposed to be in Eastern Atlantic.

0906 *Repulse to C.-in-C.*
Repulse very much regrets having to leave you at this
moment and we wish you all success in destroying
Bismarck.

0919 *From Admiralty*
Situation at 0600/25 (Positions are shown on diagram.)
(1) 1st Cruiser Squadron lost touch with enemy at 0306 in
position (shown).
(2) *Norfolk* and *Suffolk* are searching to the westward.
C.S.2 with 4 cruisers and *Victorious* is carrying out an air
and surface search to North-westward of last known enemy
position.
(3) C.-in-C. is estimated to be in the vicinity of (position
shown). *Prince of Wales* has been detached by C.S.1 to
join C.-in-C.
(4) *Rodney's* estimated position (shown).
(5) *Ramillies* estimates position (shown).
(6) *Edinburgh* estimated position (shown).
(7) *London* estimated position (shown) proceeding to search
for enemy tanker.
(8) Force H estimated position (shown) proceeding to
intercept from the southward.
(9) *Revenge* estimated position (given).
(10) *Manchester, Birmingham, Arethusa* refuelling at Hvalfjord.

0930 *From Dorsetshire*
My position with *Bulolo* and Convoy SL74 at 0930 (given).
Intend to leave convoy now and steer 065° at 25 knots to
intercept and shadow enemy.

1152 *From Commander-in-Chief German Navy to Fleet Commander
Bismarck*
*Heartiest congratulations on your birthday. May you continue to
be equally successful in this coming year.*

1313 *From Group West to Bismarck*
*7 U-boats will form patrol line between (positions given). 1
U-boat approximately in position (given).*

1414 *From Admiralty*
Convoys HX.128 and SC.32 are to reverse courses for 12 hours and then proceed on route ordered.

1424 *From Admiralty*
Ramillies is to join *Britannic* and escort her to Halifax. *Eskimo* now believed with *Britannic* is to report position, course and speed to *Britannic*.

1540 *From Prince of Wales*
Intend to proceed Hvalfjord at 2000. Estimate fuel remaining on arrival will be 6%.

1545 *From Prince of Wales*
Bismarck opened fire, range 23,000 yards just after *Hood*. Fire immediately effective on *Hood*. *Bismarck's* secondary armament opened at 20,000 yards.

1625 *From Adolf Hitler to Fleet Commander Bismarck*
Best wishes on your birthday.

1831 *From Group West*
Reference FW air reconnaissance. No enemy sighting reports.

1932 *From Group West to Bismarck*
Strong air forces available for arrival Bismarck. Battle formations up to 14° west. Patrol line in accordance with my 1313 with 5 U-boats. 3 destroyers for escort. Outer channels of Brest and St. Nazaire under control. If necessary possible to put into La Pallice as well. Report when passing 10° west.

2344 *From Group West to Bismarck*
Assume you will continue directly to French west coast harbour even if no contact with enemy.

26th May

0011 *From Admiralty*
Unless otherwise ordered by C.-in-C., one cruiser is to proceed to watch Denmark Straits and remaining two the Iceland-Faroes passage.

0036 *Admiralty to Admiral, South Africa*
Nelson is to proceed as soon as possible to Gibraltar at best speed.

0446 *From Admiral, South Africa*
Nelson expects to arrive Gibraltar 1600 Saturday 31 May.

(*Note:* During this period many signals were made organising re-fuelling of capital ships, cruisers and destroyers.)

1015 *Admiralty to* Suffolk
Proceed to search area (given) for enemy supply ships subsequently fuelling Newfoundland on relief by *Repulse*.

1025 *Group West to* Bismarck
Reconnaissance started according to plan. Weather situation in Biscay makes extended escort impossible. Therefore only close air cover possible for time being.

1030 *From Catalina aircraft*
One battleship in sight (position 4).

1052 *Force H to Ark Royal*
Do *NOT* break W/T silence.

1052 *Admiralty to Force H*
Renown is not to become engaged with *Bismarck* unless *Bismarck* is already heavily engaged by either *King George V* or *Rodney*.

1101 *Force H to Ark Royal*
Propose you fly off one or two long range shadowers now. Catalina's report may be somewhat inaccurate.

1103 *Force H to Ark Royal*
Consider we maintain present course until reconnaissance has returned when full scale striking force should be prepared.

1115 *From Ark Royal's aircraft*
One battleship in sight (position given).

(*From* 1115/26 *until* 2320/26 *Ark Royal's aircraft continuously passed signals reporting the enemy and spotting for gunnery. Destroyers of 4th flotilla shadowed and reported enemy throughout the night, and Ark Royal's aircraft were at it again from first light until* 1152/27.)

1154 *From Bismarck*
Enemy aircraft shadowing. Land plane.

1156 *From Group West*
English aircraft reports to 15th reconnaissance group at 1030: One battleship in sight (position 4).

1220 *Admiralty to submarine Severn*
Turn to Gibraltar at maximum speed to establish offensive patrol in Straits of Gibraltar in case *Bismarck* or *Prinz Eugen* endeavours to pass into Mediterranean. *Cairndale* and *City of Dieppe* are to continue in accordance with previous orders.

1228 *Admiralty to Admiral, Gibraltar*
Bismarck reported by Catalina aircraft in (position 4). Establish air and submarine patrols to prevent possible passage into Mediterranean. Patrols are to take preference over convoy duty. Spanish territorial waters need *NOT* be respected for this operation.

1315 *Force H to Sheffield*
Close and shadow enemy battleship to supplement aircraft reports.

1345 *Force H to C.-in-C.*
Enemy position course and speed (given). My position course and speed (given). *Sheffield* detached to shadow.

1424 *From Admiralty*
Repulse is to fuel as rapidly as possible and is then to reinforce *Suffolk* in operation ordered. *Prinz Eugen* may be fuelling in this area. Report probable time of leaving Newfoundland.

1520 *Force H to C.-in-C.*
Air striking force left at 1500.

1553 *From Group West*
Enemy aircraft reports to Plymouth: Have lost contact with battleship.

1559 *Force H to Victorious*
Immediately after completion of attack ask aircraft by W/T if enemy is cruiser or battleship.

1722 *Force H to Ark Royal*
Was any attack delivered.

1746 *Ark Royal to Force H*
Yes. 11 torpedoes fired at *Sheffield*. No hits. Afraid instructions to shadow not received in *Ark Royal*. Aircraft left without this knowledge. Your 1345 not decoded and shown to me until striking force had taken its departure.

1800 *Force H to C.-in-C.*
Striking force scored no hits and leaves again at 1830.

1813 *From Group West*
English aircraft regained contact at 1600.

1821 *C.-in-C. to Force H*
King George V had to reduce to 22 knots at 1705 to economise fuel. Unless enemy speed is reduced intend to return to fuel at midnight. *Rodney* can continue pursuit but without destroyer escort. Recommend you remain with carrier.

1823 *Ark Royal to Sheffield*
Striking force leaving 1850 has orders to contact you before attacking. Direct them.

1903 *From Bismarck*
Fuel situation urgent. When can I expect fuel.

1910 *Renown* sighted and challenged destroyers. They identified themselves as 4th flotilla (*Cossack, Zulu, Maori, Sikh*).

1935 *Force H to Ark Royal*
Do you think you could manage a third attack.

1940 *Ark Royal to Force H*
Intend to make an effort with 6 aircraft. All depends on time of return.

1954 *From Bismarck*
Am being attacked by carrier borne aircraft.

2015 *From Bismarck*
Ship no longer manoeuvrable.

2054 *C.-in-C. to Force H*
Request aircraft may give D4 (*Cossack*) visual link with enemy.

2056 *Admiralty to C.-in-C.*
Assume you are organising destroyer night attacks if possible. No answer required.

2105 *From Bismarck*
Approximate position (given). Torpedo hit aft.

2115 *From Bismarck*
Torpedo hit amidships.

2117 *Group West*
U-boat reports at 2000 One battleship one aircraft carrier in approximate position (given) course 115° high speed.

2140 *From Bismarck*
Ship no longer manoeuvrable. We fight to the last shell. Long live the Fuehrer.

2225 *Force H to C.-in-C.*
Torpedo bomber attack scored *one* hit amidships.

2230 *Norfolk*
My position course and speed (given). Fuel remaining 30%. Can operate with *Rodney* or Force H.

2246 *From Captain of 4th destroyer flotilla in Cossack (hereafter Cossack)*
Destroyers shadow the enemy.

2307 *Force H to Ark Royal*
Are you sending off another striking force.

2312 *Ark Royal to Force H*
No. May have 12 torpedo bombers ready for dawn attack. Suggest dawn search. A probable second hit obtained on starboard quarter in last attack.

2325 *From Bismarck*
Am surrounded by Renown and light forces.

2345 *Force H to C.-in-C.*
3rd torpedo bomber attack not possible tonight. Dawn attack tomorrow 12 aircraft. Am turning west for short distance to clear you.

2358 *From Bismarck*
To the Fuehrer of the German Reich Adolf Hitler. We fight to the last in our belief in you my Fuehrer and in the firm faith in Germany's victory.

2359 *From Bismarck*
Armament and engines still intact. Ship however cannot be steered with engines.

27th May

0001 *Admiralty*
Further examination of photographs of Brest taken on May 25th show *Scharnhorst* has moved along the wall 1 length eastward.

0002 *From Sikh*
Enemy's speed is 12 knots.

0009 *From C.-in-C.*
Enemy appears badly damaged. Intend engaging from westward at dawn.

0037 *From Admiralty*
Admiralty appreciation is that *Bismarck* intends to make for Brest.

0046 *From Force H to C.-in-C.*
After being torpedoed *Bismarck* made two complete circles and speed reduced.

0122 *Zulu*
Have delivered torpedo attack.

0138 *Maori*
Have delivered attack. Enemy making smoke.

0145 *Maori*
1 hit confirmed. Extensive fire on forecastle.

0146 *From Cossack*
Cossack attack completed. Claimed one hit.

0153 *From Adolf Hitler to the Fleet Commander Bismarck*
I thank you in the name of the German people.

From Adolf Hitler to the crew of battleship Bismarck
*The whole of Germany is with you. What can still be done will
be done. The performance of your duty will strengthen our people
in the struggle for their existence.*

0221 *From Fleet Commander Bismarck to C.-in-C. German Navy*
*Propose Lieutenant Commander Schneider, Gunnery Officer, be
awarded Knights Cross for sinking Hood.*

0234 *From Sikh*
Enemy appears to be stopped.

0305 *Force H to Ark Royal*
At what time will striking force take off. With any luck we
may finish her off before Commander-in-Chief Home Fleet
arrives.

0320 *Ark Royal to Force H*
Aircraft ready now but consider attack should not be
launched until they can differentiate between friend and foe,
shortly after 0600.

0351 *Commander-in-Chief German Navy to Lieutenant Commander
Schneider*
*The Fuehrer has awarded you the Knights Cross for sinking the
battlecruiser Hood. Heartiest congratulations.*

0355 *From Cossack*
Enemy made good 8 miles 310° between 0240 and 0340
and is still capable of heavy and accurate fire.

0633 *From Force H*
Air attack postponed. Low visibility.

0637 *Ark Royal to Force H*
In this weather our torpedo bombers may be a menace to
our ships. May I strike down aircraft please.

0707 *Force H to Ark Royal*
Yes.

0710 *From Bismarck*
Send U-boat to save War diary.

(This was the last signal made by *Bismarck*.)

0716 *Admiralty*
Bomber command is sending a striking force to position (given) by 1000 to meet possibility of a second enemy ship endeavouring to make French coast.

0940 *From Norfolk*
Vessel with suspicious marking approaching from Southward.

0942 *From Norfolk*
Renown approaching from Southward.

1025 *Force H to C.-in-C.*
Have you disposed of enemy.

1028 *C.-in-C. to Force H*
Have had to discontinue action for fuel.

1042 *C.-in-C. to Force H*
She is still afloat.

1044 *From C.-in-C.*
Any ships with torpedoes are to use them on *Bismarck*.

1045 *C.-in-C. to Force H*
Cannot sink her with guns.

Sequence of Signals from Dorsetshire
German Battleship *Bismarck* is sinking.
Enemy is sunk.
Am trying to pick up survivors.
Am picking up survivors. Too rough to lower boat. Hundreds of men in water.

1107 *From Dorsetshire*
I torpedoed *Bismarck* both sides before she sank. She had ceased firing but her colours were still flying.

1119 *From C.-in-C.*
I should like to pay the highest tribute for the most gallant fight *Bismarck* put up against impossible odds.

1322 *From Group West to Bismarck*
Reuter reports Bismarck sunk. Report situation immediately.

1514 *From Admiralty*
Their Lordships congratulate Commander-in-Chief Home
Fleet and Flag Officer Commanding Force H, and all concerned on the unrelenting pursuit and successful destruction
of the enemy's most powerful warship. The loss of *Hood*
and her company which is so deeply regretted has thus been
avenged, and the Atlantic made more secure for our trade
and that of our Allies.

From information at present available to their Lordships
there can be no doubt that had it not been for the gallant
skill and devotion to duty of the Fleet Air Arm in both
Victorious and *Ark Royal* our object might not have been
achieved.

1610 *From Admiralty to C.-in-C.*
For political reasons it is essential that nothing of the nature
of sentiments expressed in your 1119/27 should be given
publicly however much we admire a gallant fight.

7th June

1339 *From Admiralty*
Their Lordships desire to be conveyed to the wireless
personnel of H.M. ships and shore W/T stations concerned
an expression of their appreciation of the good work performed during the operations against the *Bismarck*, the
success of which depended so much on efficient wireless
communication.

RUSSIAN CONVOY
1942

The finding, fixing and sinking of the *Bismarck* was largely due
to the close co-operation between the Admiralty and the Commander-in-Chief, Home Fleet. All available forces were fitted

into the picture; nothing was left to chance. Hints were dropped, suggestions were made, but the Admiralty did not interfere with the C.-in-C. The kill was left to him. All this is readily revealed in the chain of signals relating to the operation.

The following year the pendulum swung the other way. An incident occurred in which this co-operation between the Admiralty and the man on the spot failed. Sir Winston Churchill labels it "one of the most melancholy naval episodes in the whole of the war." It led to him being asked by President Stalin if the British Navy had any sense of glory.

On 27th June, 1942, Convoy P.Q. 17, consisting of thirty-four merchant ships, sailed from Iceland to Russia. By 4th July, only four ships had been sunk after heavy air attack and the convoy was trundling along happily in calm weather, between Bear Island and the pack ice, with two-thirds of their journey behind them. In close attendance were six destroyers, two anti-aircraft ships, four corvettes and two submarines. Three cruisers and their escorting destroyers were nearby. As the day melted into endless twilight there was a lull. Even the enemy shadowing aircraft withdrew for a spell. Suddenly the Arctic peace was shattered. Not by the enemy, but by three signals which arrived from the Admiralty in quick succession:

1. 2111/4 *From Admiralty*
   Cruiser force withdraw to the westward at high speed.

2. 2123/4 *From Admiralty*
   Owing to threat from surface ships, convoy is to disperse and proceed to Russian ports.

3. 2136/4 *From Admiralty*
   Convoy is to scatter.

Those who read these signals, noted the increasing priority, and the growing alarm. They were based on information completely unknown to those with P.Q. 17, but even so scattering a convoy from 2,000 miles away was unique. A convoy is ordered to scatter when it would become an easier target to a superior enemy force by remaining concentrated. It is an "each man for himself" order. The correct way to scatter a convoy is explained in the Signal book, but it is not explained there or anywhere else how to round up a convoy once it has been scattered. It is the final and most desperate word in convoy protection. It is the prerogative of the man on the spot, when, and only when, overwhelming enemy forces have arrived on the scene. On this occasion there was no enemy present. The signals gave the ridiculous impression that the Admiralty was watching the enemy coming over P.Q. 17's horizon.

The three signals were sent because the Admiralty believed *Tirpitz*, *Hipper* and *Scheer* were on the point of leaving their base in Northern Norway to attack the convoy. The German ships did not in fact sail until 1430 on the following afternoon. When they got to sea they received reports that P.Q. 17 had scattered. Satisfied that those merchant ships had been delivered into the hands of their U-boats and bombers, they turned back. Only eleven ships out of the original thirty-four eventually struggled into Archangel.

It has been said that the ships guarding P.Q. 17 were never intended to engage heavy enemy forces. In that case why were they there? Other convoy escorts have proved what can be done in this respect against fantastic odds.

It seems that wireless telegraphy came forty years too soon for P.Q. 17. Without those three signals, whatever else might have happened, it would not have become a melancholy naval episode.

FORCE K

1941

One of the complications of war is that ships hardly ever manage to operate together for any length of time. On the rare occasions that they do their united efficiency soon becomes manifest. One of the ways it shows is by silence. Strange ships have to talk to one another, instructing, reporting, arguing. In a seasoned squadron, everyone knows the form, which eases the load on the signalmen.

Force K consisted of the cruisers *Aurora* and *Penelope*, and the destroyers *Lance* and *Lively*. They worked well and they worked frequently together, molesting the convoys carrying supplies across the Mediterranean to Rommel. No collector of signals would need to leave much space for Force K.

On 8th November, 1941, Force K sailed from Malta to intercept a convoy reported by aircraft. At 40 minutes past midnight the convoy was spotted seven miles away in the moonlight. It was escorted by four destroyers. The Force K rules were to keep in line ahead, and to engage escorts first. As they swept up and down the lines of the convoy *Aurora* alone engaged seventeen targets in 45 minutes. At 0206 Force K withdrew, having estimated their bag as two destroyers, ten merchant ships sunk, two destroyers damaged. Their own casualties amounted to five canaries which died of fright in *Penelope*. During the whole of this neat clear-cut operation only three signals were made.

GENERAL ALARM AND THE BEARING OF THE ENEMY.

REDUCE SPEED TO 20 KNOTS

DO NOT WASTE AMMUNITION

After the operation *Penelope* signalled to *Aurora*:

CONGRATULATIONS TO AURORA ON HER MAGNIFICENT BOREALIS

The Italian air force attacked Force K on its return to Malta and inflicted "wishful" damage. After this had been reported in the Italian Press Force K received the following signal from Vice Admiral, Malta:

It is with great regret that I learn from the Italian Press that one of the cruisers received 2 hits and a destroyer 1 hit during torpedo bombing. I can only think in view of the lack of damage I saw today that the Dockyard is more efficient than I thought or your camouflage is excellent.

Force K composed the following reply to Vice Admiral, Malta:

> There was an air wap from Taranto
> Who set out for exploits gallanto
> He sunka da cruise
> And get in da nooze
> To make up for da kick in da panto.

SIGNAL IK
1941

The Hamburg-Amerika cargo/passenger liner *Steiermark* (9,400 tons) was fitted out as a commerce raider and rechristened *Kormoran*. On 19th November, 1941, off the coast of Western Australia, she sighted a cruiser. *Kormoran* turned away immediately, increased to full speed and reported "a disguised raider" in sight. She made the signal as if it had come from the Dutch ship, *Straat Malakka*, whom she closely resembled.

The cruiser, H.M.A.S. *Sydney*, approached eventually to a range of one mile. At this distance *Kormoran's* Captain saw *Sydney* hoist a two-flag signal which he did not understand. He answered it with the order, "Down screens, open fire." A fierce battle followed and both ships were badly damaged. Towards evening *Sydney* steamed away under a dense cloud of smoke and was never seen again. Just before midnight *Kormoran* was abandoned and scuttled. The signal which *Sydney* hoisted was:

I.K.

(You should prepare for a hurricane or typhoon)

NOCTURNE IN V MINOR
1945

Narrative

The above title was appropriately given to an encounter between our "V" Class destroyers and a Japanese cruiser on the night of the 15/16th May, 1945.

The 26th Destroyer Flotilla, consisting of *Venus, Vigilant, Virago,* and *Verulam,* led by Captain M. L. Power in *Saumarez,* were at sea with the Fleet. On the previous night the Admiral got news that some Japanese merchant ships were at large. The 26th Flotilla were ordered to search for them.

At 10 o'clock on the morning of the 15th 'planes from the carriers spotted the enemy convoy about 150 miles to the Eastward. Operations like this in which various forces combine have to have their own label. This one was called MITRE.

The destroyers were off on the scent of the convoy when, at 1150 came the startling news that a Japanese heavy Cruiser, *Haguro,* and a destroyer had been sighted in the same area. The Merchant ships were forgotten. Operation MITRE was cancelled. Captain Power had an unpleasant moment thinking this meant that he was being recalled. The Rear Admiral commanding the 5th Cruiser Squadron soon made it clear that there was no such intention. On went the destroyers, spreading out on to a line of search as they settled down to a speed of 27 knots. They had the whole day in front of them.

Fresh information confirmed the types of enemy ships, and indicated that, having been spotted, they had deserted their convoy and turned Southward towards the protected water of the Malacca Straits. If the Flotilla intercepted this escorted cruiser before dark the odds would be on her side, for she was heavily armed with 8-in. guns with double the range of the destroyers' armament. If they did not make their best speed the enemy would

Signals

Throughout these signals

D 26 addresses Captain Power, commanding the 26th Destroyer Flotilla.

C-in-CEI   ,,   Commander-in-Chief East Indies.

B. S. 3   ,,   Admiral commanding the 3rd Battle Squadron.

C. S. 5   ,,   Rear Admiral commanding 5th Cruiser Squadron.

(R) means the signal is repeated to the addressees shown.

15th May

0217 *From BS3 to D26*
ATTACKING FORCE DESTROYERS RAISE STEAM FOR FULL SPEED FORTHWITH

0237 *From BS3 to D26*
PROCEED FORTHWITH WITH 26TH D.F. AT 27 KNOTS TO SEARCH FOR ENEMY AUXILIARY VESSEL. RETURN BY SAME ROUTE. AIR SEARCH AND STRIKE FROM CARRIERS WILL BE ARRANGED

0311 *From BS3 to D26*
IF CANCEL MITRE RECEIVED FROM C–IN–CEI OR BS3 REJOIN ME

1000   AIRCRAFT B REPORTS ATTACKING 2 ENEMY MERCHANT VESSELS IN POSITION (given)

1041 *From C-in-CEI to D26*
CANCEL MITRE REPEAT CANCEL MITRE

1056 *From D26 to CS5*
REFERENCE C–IN–CEI'S 1041 REQUEST CONFIRMATION OF CANCELLATION IN VIEW OF AIRCRAFT B REPORT

escape. For the moment there was nothing to do but remember the old motto of the Rugger field, "go for the corner flag."

Further reports during the afternoon gave Captain Power no reason to alter his plans. Towards evening, without fuss or bother, he spread his ships on a new line across the approaching course of the enemy.

As the sun went down astern of the destroyers in a blaze of colour, the sea appeared deserted except for the distant coast of Sumatra away to starboard. The destroyers raced eagerly into the approaching darkness. By 7 p.m. the Cruiser was estimated to be about 75 miles to the North-eastward and, as far as they knew, unaware of their presence.

Steaming at that speed, however, very soon introduces a fuel problem. By nightfall Captain Power realised he could do little more than sweep down to the Malayan Coast south of Penang. If he made no contact he would have to turn round and sweep back. He had no intention of being caught close to enemy airfields at dawn.

The night was dark with heavy storm clouds and rain squalls. The destroyers were pinning all their hopes on radar search. But these were the very conditions when radar played tricks. By 10 p.m. the crews had been at action stations for 12 hours and were feeling the strain a bit. By 10.30 the thought began to occur that they might be drawing a blank. Then, at 10.45 *Venus*, the most northerly ship, reported a radar contact. At first it was treated with caution; but *Venus* was persistent. Now that it was dark Captain Power had no fear of the result if only he could find the foe. He had a well trained team who knew each other's form well. There was no fear of confusion or lack of understanding. The reported contact certainly fitted in with the plot. He turned his ships towards it. At three minutes past midnight the contact was confirmed by *Saumarez*.

Radar showed a second smaller contact astern of the first—that would be the destroyer. The Flotilla turned to a parallel course and reduced speed to get into their shadowing sectors. When the range had closed to 10 miles the enemy started manœuvring freely, giving the impression that he was aware of the destroyers. Perhaps he thought they were friendly, coming as they were

1101 *From D26 to Destroyers*
HAVE BEEN RECALLED. CAN AFFORD TO EASE DOWN A BIT
PENDING REPLY TO MY APPLICATION TO CONTINUE

1150 *From Aircraft G*
ONE CRUISER ONE DESTROYER IN POSITION (given)

1155 *From CS5 to D26 (R) BS3, C-in-CEI*
REFERENCE C-IN-CEI'S 1041 YOU SHOULD SINK ENEMY SHIPS
BEFORE RETURNING

1221 *From D26 to BS3*
MY POSITION IS XXXX AM CLOSING ENEMY WARSHIPS AT
27 KNOTS

1228 *From Aircraft G*
COURSE AND SPEED OF ONE ENEMY CRUISER AND ONE
DESTROYER ARE (given) TYPE OF ENEMY REPORTED ARE ONE
NACHI CRUISER ONE MINNEKAZE DESTROYER

1252 *From CS5 to C-in-CEI (R) D26*
AM PROCEEDING TO SUPPORT D26

1254 *From D26 to Destroyers*
IF REPORTS OF ENEMY CONTINUE GOOD I SHALL PROBABLY
CONCENTRATE BEFORE CONTACT. ON SIGHTING AIM IS TO
SHADOW AND CONCENTRATE TO SOUTHWARD

1330 *From D26 to CS5 (R) BS3*
MY POSITION COURSE AND SPEED ARE (given) INTEND TO
INTERCEPT AND ATTACK BY NIGHT

1513 *From D26 to Destroyers*
IF CONTACT IS MADE IN DAYLIGHT KEEP OUT OF GUN RANGE.
TRY TO DRAW ENEMY WESTWARD, KEEPING AS FAR SOUTH AS
POSSIBLE. ATTACK BY NIGHT WILL PROBABLY BE SIMULTANE-
OUSLY FROM DIVERGENT BEARINGS OWING TO ENEMY'S LARGE
TORPEDO ARMAMENT

1551 *From Aircraft*
ONE ENEMY CRUISER AND DESTROYER IN POSITION (given)

1640 *From Aircraft*
HAVE ATTACKED ENEMY CRUISER WITH BOMBS RESULT OF
ATTACK PROBABLE HITS

from the direction of Singapore. That would be the last quarter from which he would expect attack.

Captain Power decided to attack at 1 a.m. At ten minutes to, the situation shaped exactly according to plan. The net was spread and the quarry was steaming into it at a relative speed of 50 m.p.h.

Then events moved fast. The Cruiser turned away to the North-west, spoiling the attack. The Flotilla chased after her, *Venus* bearing down from the Northward. *Saumarez* went "hard over" to avoid colliding with the Japanese destroyer, and opened fire.

The Cruiser replied with everything she had. Near misses drenched everyone on *Saumarez's* bridge. One shell tore its way through her funnel. Then, a direct hit amidships. A blow, a list, escaping steam, and the lights went out. But before this she had got all her torpedoes off at the massive shape as it slid by less than a mile away. On came the lights and away limped *Saumarez* to sort things out behind a smoke screen. Meanwhile other attacks were being pressed home on the Cruiser. Three white plumes of exploding torpedoes were seen. Then a violent explosion from another direction. *Saumarez* thought it was one of the Flotilla. The rest of the Flotilla thought it was *Saumarez*. As Captain Power observed afterwards, "The rest of the Flotilla saw it and apparently eagerly assumed that this marked the end of yet another dictator. Happily, such was not the case." A burst of star shell over *Saumarez* was followed by a report from one destroyer,

AM ILLUMINATING THE ENEMY

The rather cold, though welcome voice of Captain Power replied,

THINK THAT IS ME

Events slowed down a little. *Saumarez* had taken nothing worse than a knock in No. 1 boiler room. The mysterious explosion had almost certainly been the Jap destroyer, stopping someone's torpedo. At 1.30 *Virago* reported the Cruiser's upper deck awash. By then her guns were almost silenced. *Saumarez* lay in the deep field, quite restored and doubtless anxious to join in the final sacrificial rites, but wisely clear of the stray torpedoes which were speeding about in the cruiser's vicinity. Captain Power stayed where he was until he received the report

CRUISER SUNK

after which he formed up his Flotilla and led them home.

1647 *From D26 to Verulam and Vigilant*
DONT BUST YOURSELVES

1648 *From D26 to Verulam and Vigilant*
I AM AIMING TO SPREAD BY DARK AND THEN CARRY OUT
CROSS SEARCH. VIRAGO AND VENUS WILL PROLONG THE LINE
THE OTHER SIDE OF ME

1651 *From D26 to Virago and Venus*
FORM ON A LINE OF BEARING (given) FROM ME IN SEQUENCE
VIRAGO VENUS DISTANCE BETWEEN SHIPS 4 MILES

1811 *From D26 to Destroyers*
FAILING FURTHER REPORT INTEND TO REMAIN ON PRESENT
COURSE AND SPEED UNTIL MIDNIGHT. AT THAT TIME INTEND
TO REVERSE COURSE AND REDUCE TO 20 KNOTS WITHOUT
FURTHER SIGNAL

2345 *From D26*
VESSEL SIZE UNKNOWN DETECTED BY R.D.F.

16th May

0125 *From D26*
AM ENGAGING ENEMY

0140 *From D26 to C-in-CEI*
CRUISER SINKING

0210 *From D26 to Destroyers*
V'S FOR VICTORY PICK UP PRISONERS STAY NO LONGER
THAN 10 MINUTES

0212 *From D26 to Destroyers*
ON LIGHTS. JOIN ME AT FULL SPEED

From D26 to C-in-CEI (R) CS5
MY POSITION COURSE AND SPEED (given). ENEMY CRUISER
SUNK. DESTROYER NOT ACCOUNTED FOR. ONE BOILER ROOM
OUT OF ACTION IN SAUMAREZ. REMAINDER OF FLOTILLA NOT
DAMAGED.

The last paragraph of his report on this brilliant encounter reads as follows:

"The attack was a success; but it was by no means a perfect and polished performance. There is much to be learnt from it, and plenty of room for improvement. The errors and omissions, mostly on my part in the control, were made up for by team work and enthusiasm. The result left me proud of the entire command."

SHIPS THAT PASSED
1953-54

The great attraction about the Royal Tour of 1953-4 to Australia was the warmth and friendliness shown to and by The Queen and Prince Philip. This was best revealed in the film. An equally charming but less public record of the Tour comes from the pages of the signal logs of H.M. yachts *Gothic* and *Britannia*. They contain a collection of signals from people in liners, tankers and freighters who passed the Royal convoy at sea on its 17,000 mile journey. None of them actually saw the Queen but their greetings are just as warm as those pictured on the cinema screen. These logs contain the Merchant Navy's private share in the Tour.

Ships passing at sea are as a rule mildly curious about one another. Each likes to know where the other is from and whither

1212 *From CS5 to D26*

    HEARTIEST CONGRATULATIONS ON THE VERY THOROUGH WAY IN WHICH YOU DEALT WITH MY 1155/15*

    (* YOU SHOULD SINK ENEMY SHIPS BEFORE RETURNING)

From C-in-CEI to D26

    BEST CONGRATULATIONS TO EVERYONE. D26 SHOWED GRAND FORM IN DESIGN AND EXECUTION

---

bound. Meeting the Royal Yacht in mid-ocean was different. When distant specks grew into gleaming ships with standard and ensigns floating there was only one thing to be done, and that was to make a signal.

One can imagine waste paper baskets filling as the ships approached one another. Drafting a signal to a Queen cannot be taken lightly, but although the senders were so far separated it is interesting to note the similarity in the eventual wording of these messages.

Humble duty, loyal greetings, and Bon voyage appeared most frequently. They came from nineteen thousand passengers, officers and crew homeward bound from Australia in the 28,000 ton Orient liner *Orcades*. In a smaller voice the Captain of the 2,500 ton British tanker *Crista* signalled:

> My officers join my wife and myself in sending loyal greetings to your Majesty. We wish you a pleasant voyage and a safe happy return home.

Between these tonnages there is a long list of ships of all shapes and sizes who sent signals. From the 1,400 ton Dutch Motor Ship *Ruys* came:

> I, my officers, and all British passengers being together with your Majesty in the Indian Ocean wish to convey our respects and our best wishes for your happy return voyage on your wonderful trip round the world.

The 7,000 ton British India passenger ship *Pentakota* said:

> Greetings and a message of loyalty and devotion. Bon voyage and happy home-coming from all on board.

The 1st Battalion of the Gordon Highlanders homeward bound from the jungles of Malaya offered their loyal greetings from H.M. Transport *Empire Fowey*. The 8,000 ton passenger cargo ship *Clytonens* remembered another occasion to celebrate:

> Loyal hearty greetings. We also toast your Majesty on this your birthday.

William Gwalkley, a large British Tanker on her maiden voyage, sent good wishes from Latitude 0412 North, Longitude 8730 East.

Biggest of all was the 30,000 ton Orient liner *Orsova*, also on her maiden voyage to Australia. From her the Commodore sent a message on 5th April personally to Prince Philip.

> . . . It is tactful of *Orsova* to pay her court tonight in darkness because night will conceal the new funnel which has a Welsh hat on top. We are anxious to conceal the regrettable fact that we cannot raise it in salute. Respect and greetings.

His Royal Highness composed the following reply:

Hat shapes and sizes
May win no first prizes
But our pride and strength grows
With new ships and cargoes.

Philip.

To the long list of similar signals from proud ships may be added the passing wishes of Horace Brindesmead, probably the first airliner to send such a signal. Later on she was to carry the Royal couple for many miles of their tour.

Each ship, and this airliner, received a reply from Her Majesty expressing her thanks.

In addition to these signals from the Merchant Navy there were others made by the Queen during the Royal Tour to the naval ships and aircraft which formed her escort.

From Flag Officer Commanding Royal Yachts to H.M.S. Black Prince (New Zealand cruiser escort)
I have to convey the following message. Since you came to meet us in Mid-Pacific you have had manifold duties to perform but whether at sea, or on duty ashore, I have been delighted with all that I have seen you do. I was particularly pleased to have been able to visit your ship and meet your officers and men. Goodbye and thank you very much. Elizabeth R.

From Flag Officer Royal Yachts to H.M.S. Ceylon
I have to convey to you the following message: Thank you for your escort from Fremantle and I am glad you were able to pay some visits beforehand in Australia. I was pleased to be able to visit your officers and ship's company and thought that the arrangements for my visit were admirable. Goodbye and good luck. Elizabeth R.

From Flag Officer Royal Yachts to Sunderland Aircraft
I have to convey the following message from the Queen:
Thank you for your escort.

On a particular occasion the Australian Commander-in-Chief arranged to have the ship's company of the aircraft carrier *Vengeance* fallen in on the flight deck to form an aerial view of the Royal signature. In due course, and in a lighter vein the following signal was made.

From Flag Officer Royal Yachts to Flag Officer Commanding the Australian Fleet
I have to convey the following message from the Queen:
Thank you for your original forgery.

Here is Her Majesty's farewell signal to the Australian Navy.

From Flag Officer Royal Yachts to Flag Officer Australian Fleet
I have to convey the following message.
Thank you so much for all the arrangements you have made and the facilities you have provided during my visit to Australia, in particular on the Queensland Coast. I leave you now, happy in the knowledge that the Australian Fleet is in your good hands and in splendid heart. Goodbye and please tell them what I said. Elizabeth R.

The following message has been passed to the Royal Australian Navy: Her Majesty the Queen graciously commands, Splice the Main Brace.

Within the Royal Tour itself, birthday wishes to Her Majesty were expressed in the following signals, made while *Britannia* was on passage from England to Tobruk:

19/4 *From Britannia's Captain to Flag Officer Royal Yachts*
Should you consider it appropriate would you please convey

on Wednesday to Her Majesty the Queen my humble duty and loyal good wishes of the officers and Royal Yachtsmen of *Britannia*. Many happy returns of the day. The captain of H.M.S. *Loch Alvie* has asked if he, his officers and ship's company may join in any messages I send in view of the contribution *Loch Alvie* has made to our trip in providing escort (not to mention Easter Eggs).

May I add that we are deeply conscious of the great privilege we have in conveying Their Royal Highnesses on this maiden voyage.

21/4 *From Flag Officer Royal Yachts to Britannia*
I have to convey to you the following message. I send the officers and Royal Yachtsmen of *Britannia* and the officers and ratings of *Loch Alvie* my sincere thanks for their loyal message on my birthday which I have received with much pleasure.

Regarding the Royal children, *Britannia* had already made a reassuring signal about them on her departure from England.

From Britannia to Flag Officer Royal Yachts
Just cleared Portland and on our way. Both Royal children in cracking form. Sun shining and a following wind.

Two days previously, another signal from the opposite side of the world shows that they were not overlooked by the Royal Australian Navy:

From Flag Officer Royal Yachts to Vengeance
I have to convey the following message.
I am most grateful for the two lovely boxes which you have given me for my children. I know they will be thrilled. Thank you very much. Elizabeth R.

And finally, from Admiral Earl Mountbatten:

> *From Commander-in-Chief, Mediterranean, personal for H.M.*
> *The Queen*
>
> Edwina and I have just seen Charles and Anne, who are very
> well and send much love. Charles has invited us to go on a
> picnic with him tomorrow.

IV

Scrap Log

From now on the reader is faced with a scrapbook—Scrap Log would describe it better—of individual signals.

In the day's work a great deal is said which is not worth recording. So with signals. Most of them are either technical, routine, or just plain dull. Out of the two-hundred odd tons of signals sent during World War II, a mere truckload would cover exciting or interesting episodes of which a handful would be outstanding. Yet, both in war and peace, occasionally there flashes from a lamp or crackles from an aerial a gem which is worth preserving. Some of these may have taken time to compose, others came straight off the cuff. Some are serious; some are humorous and, of those, a few are funny only at the receiving end. Can any originator, for example, have felt less flippant than the one who sent: SOS. SOS. MAID OF CORK SINKING?

The selection which follows could appear under such headings as: Inspiring, Sarcastic, Witty. But they do not seem to take kindly to grouping; therefore they have been thoroughly mixed up. Without mercy, the reader is jerked from situation to situation. At one moment he is in a sea battle; the next he may be on a peacetime picnic. The point to remember is that the situations are real; they all really happened.

DECLARING WARS, CONCLUDING THEM, AND TIDYING UP AFTERWARDS— BY SIGNAL

These few signals are taken from a very large selection of those made round about the declarations and armistices of the two

World Wars. Some of them are historic. Others are of little importance, except to show different aspects of the "gear-change" which takes place from Peace time to War and back again.

The Beginning of World War I

3/8/14   *From Admiralty to destroyer flotilla at sea*
British ultimatum to Germany expires at 2300.
From Admiralty
Commence hostilities with Germany.
From Flotilla Leader
Importance of wearing clean underclothes in action is stressed. This may make all the difference between a clean and a suppurating wound.

4/8/14   *From His Majesty King George V to Admiral Sir John Jellicoe, C.-in-C. Grand Fleet*
At this grave moment in our national history I send to you and through you to the officers and men of the fleets of which you have assumed command, the assurance of my confidence that under your direction they will revive and renew the old glories of the Royal Navy, and prove once again the sure shield of Britain and her Empire in the hour of trial.
                           George RI

A lieutenant in Command of a refitting destroyer returned from a yachting cruise p.m. 4th August, 1914. On arrival on board he sent for the Signal Log. He waded through all the routine signals about ships' movements, exercise programmes, Sunday church parties, changes in personnel, cricket matches. Slowly he brought his mind back from the limited horizon of his 10 ton yawl. Staring at him from the log was General Signal from Admiralty which read:
Commence hostilities with Germany.

5/8/14   *From Admiralty*
Following are transferred from conditional to absolute

contraband: Aeroplanes, Airships, Balloons and aircraft of all kinds and their component parts together with accessories and articles for use in connection with Balloons and aircraft.

5/8/14 *From Admiralty to C.-in-C. Med.*
Austria has not declared war against France or England. Continue watching Adriatic for double purpose of preventing Austrians from emerging unobserved and preventing Germans entering.

6/8/14 *From Admiralty to Bacchante*
German Ambassador leaving Harwich today in Great Eastern Steamer *St. Petersburg*

7/8/14 *From Admiralty to Bacchante*
British Ambassador from Berlin returning Hook of Holland in Great Eastern Steamer *St. Petersburg*. She leaves between 4 and 5 p.m. today.

(It is reassuring to know Great Eastern Steamer *St. Petersburg* ended up on the right side.)

U.S.A. Declares War

7/4/17 *From British Ambassador, Washington*
War Resolution passed by Congress was signed by President this afternoon. Proclamation also issued that a state of war exists between United States and German Government, and establishing regulations to ensure good behaviour of alien enemies.

The End of World War I

7/11/18 *From Chief of Naval Staff to Admiralty*
Am leaving for unknown destination with Marshal Foch this afternoon.

9/11/18 *From German Imperial Chancellor Prince Max of Baden*
The Kaiser and King has decided to renounce the throne. The Imperial Chancellor will remain in office until the questions connected with the abdication of the Kaiser, the renouncing of the throne of the German Empire and of Prussia and the setting up of a Regency has been settled.

11/11/18 *From Admiralty*
The Armistice is signed. Hostilities are to be suspended forthwith. All anti-submarine defensive measures for the security of men-of-war at sea or in harbour are to remain in force until further orders. Submarines on the surface are not to be attacked unless their hostile intentions are obvious.

(As someone pointed out, this meant waiting until you were torpedoed to find out.)

11/11/18 *From Commander-in-Chief, Grand Fleet to Admiralty*
It is not the custom for H.M. ships to dress ship except on ceremonial occasions. . . . The traditional method of celebrating an auspicious occasion is to splice the main brace and I have given orders to that effect.

11/11/18 *From His Majesty King George V to the First Lord of the Admiralty*
Now that the last and most formidable of our enemies has acknowledged the triumph of the Allied Arms on behalf of Right and Justice, I wish to express my praise and thankfulness to the officers and men of the Royal Navy and Marines, with their comrades of the Fleet Auxiliaries and Mercantile Marine who for more than four years have kept open the seas, protected our shores and given us safety.

Ever since that fateful 4 August 1914, I have remained steadfast in my confidence that whether fortune frowned or smiled the Royal Navy would once more prove the sure shield of the British Empire in the hour of trial.

Never in its history has the Royal Navy, with God's help, done greater things for us, nor better sustained its old glories and the chivalries of the seas. With full and grateful hearts the Peoples of the British Empire salute the White, the Red, and the Blue Ensigns and those who have given their lives for the flag. I am proud to have served in the Navy. I am prouder still to be its head on this memorable day.

GEORGE R.I.

12/11/18 *From Admiralty*

The Lords Commissioners of the Admiralty desire heartily to congratulate officers and men of the Royal Navy and Royal Marines upon the triumph of the Allied cause, in realisation of which they have played so splendid a part, adding lustre throughout to the great tradition of the Service to which they belong.

Their Lordships feel that after four years of ceaseless vigilance a relaxation of war conditions cannot but be eagerly desired by officers and men and they may be relied upon to grant leave and modify routine immediately when circumstances permit. For the present however with German submarines possibly still at sea ignorant of the Armistice, with the work of escorting ships to be surrendered or interned devolving largely on British Navy and with the full capacity of the minesweepers required for clearing the seas it is plain that no officer or man can be spared from their duties until the safety of the country at sea is assured.

The Navy had in time of Peace to be ready for War in a sense which land forces cannot be. Now that Peace is again in prospect, it may prove that even after the troops in the field are enjoying a relief from tension the Navy must for a time continue its war routine. If so their Lordships are confident that this will be cheerfully accepted as being at once the burden and the privilege of the Empire's first line of defence.

From Commander-in-Chief, Grand Fleet (Admiral Beatty) after the surrendered German Fleet had anchored.

21/11/18 THE GERMAN FLAG WILL BE HAULED DOWN AT SUNSET TODAY AND NOT HOISTED AGAIN WITHOUT PERMISSION.

The Beginning of World War II

1/9/39   *From Admiralty*
The use of sirens and hooters is prohibited except for air raid warnings. The sounding of sirens or whistles in ships which might be heard on land is to be restricted to the minimum necessary for the safety of navigation.

3/9/39   *From Commander-in-Chief, Portsmouth*
All concerned at Home and Abroad from Admiralty. Commence hostilities at once with Germany.

3/9/39   *From Admiralty*
Winston is back.

3/9/39   *From Admiralty*
Immediate. Special telegram TOTAL Germany.

3/9/39   *From Admiralty*
All available destroyers at Rosyth are to proceed to sea and steer NNE with moderate despatch.

3/9/39   *From Admiralty to Admiral Commanding 2nd Cruiser Squadron*
Steer North East at Full Speed.

5/9/39   *From Admiralty to C.-in-C. Home Fleet*
A general issue of life-saving belts has not been contemplated but arrangements are now being made to obtain supplies and secure the most rapid production practicable.

170

5/9/39   *From C.-in-C. Home Fleet to Admiralty*
Request the latest information as to number of long distance bombers Germany possesses.

6/9/39   *From Admiralty*
Special telegram FISHING 3 September FORECASTLE all areas PUGILIST WINCH DOVER.

6/9/39   *From Admiralty to destroyers Jackal, Janus, Juno*
British Embassy party from Berlin will be leaving Rotterdam in S.S. *Batavia V* at 0500 tomorrow Thursday. *Jackal, Janus* and *Juno* are to rendezvous with S.S. *Batavia V* in position 130 degrees 4 miles from Maas light vessel and escort her to the Tongue light vessel.

6/9/39   *From C.in-C. Home Fleet to Admiralty*
At present the navigation lights at Copensay, Pentland Skerries, Stroma and Swona in Orkney Islands cannot be controlled from the base and it is requested that immediate steps are taken to rectify this. . . . This is a matter affecting the safety of H.M. ships and I trust it will receive their Lordships' early attention. My first communication on this subject was dated 27 September 1938.

Autumn 1939   *From Admiralty to Destroyer*
Proceed with all despatch.

From Destroyer to Admiralty
Request destination.

From Admiralty to Destroyer
Aden, repeat Aden.

From Destroyer to Admiralty
Am at Aden.

9/9/39   *From Admiralty to C.-in-C. Home Fleet*
It is suggested that if practicable the force now in Icelandic waters might look into Denmark Strait and report if any considerable quantity of shipping is avoiding contraband control by using this channel.

The End of World War II

11/9/43   *From Commander-in-Chief Mediterranean to Admiralty:*
BE PLEASED TO INFORM THEIR LORDSHIPS THAT THE ITALIAN
BATTLE FLEET NOW LIES AT ANCHOR UNDER THE GUNS OF
THE FORTRESS OF MALTA.

7/5/45   *From SHAEF, signed Eisenhower*
A representative of the German High Command signed
the unconditional surrender of all German land, sea and
air forces in Europe to the Allied Expeditionary Force
and simultaneously to the Soviet Command at 0141
hours Central European Time 7 May, under which all
forces will cease active operations at 0001 hours 9 May.

7/5/45   *From Admiralty*
Cease attack on ALL repetition ALL shipping. Attacks on
U-boats should continue as heretofore.

7/5/45   *From Admiralty*
A 3-day course of instruction for resettlement information for officers is being held. . . .

8/5/45   *From C.-in-C. Home Fleet to Home Fleet*
For many months I have watched with admiration and
pride the officers and men of the Home Fleet carrying
out their many arduous and often monotonous tasks
with unfailing zeal and thoroughness. Now at last
victory has come without giving the chance of bringing
the enemy fleet to action at sea, but the very fact that he
has allowed his ships to be put out of action separately
in harbour is of great tribute to the way in which the
Home Fleet has carried out its task. Ships of the Home
Fleet may be called on to carry out tasks to help in the
settlement of Europe in the near future and I have no
doubt that you will tackle these with similar efficiency
and enthusiasm. I wish to convey my congratulations
and thanks to all officers and men who have served so
well in the Home Fleet.

9/5/45   *From Vice Admiral Lemounier to 1st Sea Lord*
En ce jour qui consacre la victoire totale sur L'Allemagne
je vous exprime en mon nom et en celui des officiers et
marins Francais nos sentiments de profonde admiration
pour l'oeuvre formidable accomplie par la marine
Britannique dans la lutte contre l'ennemi commun, pour
la maîtrise des mers et lors des grands débarquements qui
ont permis la libération de la France. Les Marins
Francais ont été fiers de prendre leur part dans cette lutte
aux côtés de leurs camarades des marins Alliés. Les
succes remportés dans cet hemisphère garantissent le
rapide et complet succes dans la lutte en extrème-Orient
contre le dernier adversaire.

13/5/45   *From Admiralty*
S.S. *Scythia* has been allocated to convey the Norwegian
government to Norway. The party will consist of about
700 men and 150 women.

From C.-in-C. Fifth Fleet to Fifth Fleet Pacific
The war with Japan will end at 1200 on 15th August.
It is likely that Kamikazes will attack the fleet after this
time as a final fling. Any ex-enemy aircraft attacking the
fleet is to be shot down in a friendly manner.

19/7/45   *From Commander-in-Chief*
Effective upon signing of Japanese surrender terms propose discontinue all combat areas.

From Admiralty to B.A.D. Washington
In view of the end of the war it is intended to propose
at the conference in September that the whole world
should be declared a non-combat area.

Late 1945. A Trawler passes close to a Cruiser. The Trawler's
crew are in various interpretations of naval uniform and they
pay no attention to the Cruiser whatever.

From Cruiser to Trawler:
Why no marks of respect.
Reply from Trawler:
Release Group 22 (next day).

SCRAP LOG—GENERAL

Perhaps the most exciting moment in a warship is on sighting the enemy and signalling the sighting report. However much it may have been anticipated, the actual moment when it happens has a thrill of its own.

On 31st May, 1916, *Southampton*, flagship of the 2nd Light Cruiser Squadron, was stationed ahead of our Battle Cruisers. It was a fine afternoon; the sea calm, the sun shining through patches of haze. Though the advanced forces had brushed against one another, *Southampton* had taken no part and touch with the enemy had now been lost. The guns' crews were relaxed, the men chatting and smoking; everything seemed quiet and peaceful.

Suddenly, from the foretop, a ship was reported ahead. In a few minutes the German High Seas Fleet could be distinguished. The shutter on the signalling searchlight began clacking. *Southampton* signalled to *Lion*, Admiral Beatty's flagship:

> SIGHTED ENEMYS BATTLE FLEET ON BEARING SOUTH-EAST COURSE OF ENEMY NORTH.

From Fleetwood to C.-in-C. Portsmouth
> HAVE ONE COLORADO BEETLE ON BOARD. REQUEST DISPOSAL.

Two submarines were returning to harbour after the annual inspection by their Admiral, Rear Admiral Dent. He was embarked in one of the submarines and had just retired from the bridge. During the inspection the submarines had to carry out an attack on a battleship, firing a torpedo with a crushable head. After attacking, each submarine recovered its own torpedo and lashed it to the casing. The submarine carrying the Admiral had obviously scored a hit for the head of their torpedo was well crushed. There was no visible damage to the 2nd submarine's torpedo. The following signals were exchanged.

From 1st submarine (with Admiral) to 2nd submarine:
DID YOU GET A HIT.

From 2nd submarine:
YES, DENT IS IN THE HEAD BELOW.

From 1st submarine:
HOW DID YOU GUESS.

This contribution from an ex-Signal Bos'n is typical of the keenness of the signal branch between the wars.

"We were lying at Argostoli with all the Mediterranean Fleet. I was in the *Royal Oak* at the time and there was quite a bit of friendly sniping going on. I had caught Barham twice in half an hour before 0930. I then received the following from Fleet Signal Officer:

I HOPE THAT YOUR ADMIRAL IS WELL.

"On investigation I found to my horror that the Admiral's flag was at half mast. I think that is the best one that I was ever caught on."

From Gracie Fields (trawler):
GRACIE FIELDS MAKING WATER AND SINKING FAST.

Destroyer flotilla at sea, time 2100. No. 2 destroyer seems to be keeping much too close to the stern of her leader.

From Flotilla leader to No. 2:
WOULD YOU CARE TO JOIN ME IN A GLASS OF PORT.

Our light forces were on a sweep in the Skaggerak in World War I in hazy weather. Shortly after dawn the most northerly cruiser signalled:
ENEMY BATTLESHIP BEARING NNE DISTANCE 2 MILES. AM PREPARING TO RAM.

Later came:
CANCEL MY LAST SIGNAL. BATTLESHIP TURNS OUT TO BE A LIGHTHOUSE.

(The lighthouses on the northern shores of the Skaggerak often have twin towers and outhouses which look like superstructure and turrets.)

From Salvage tug to C.-in-C. Plymouth:
HAVE ONE HAND WITH SEPTIC FOOT.

From Ship to Ship:
PLEASE SEND YOUR TECHNICAL EXPERT TO SEE OUR FOREMOST GUN.
Reply:
OUR TECHNICAL EXPERT CAN SEE YOUR FOREMOST GUN FROM HERE.

From C.-in-C. Mediterranean, to Cardiff:
> YOUR CONFIDENTIAL BOOK OFFICER IS TO REPORT AT MY
> OFFICE FOR DESTRUCTION.

1059/10/12/44. From Senior Naval Officer afloat—General:
> SHIPS ARE TO DRESS WITH MASTHEAD FLAGS IN HONOUR OF
> HIS MAJESTY'S ASCENSION TOMORROW MONDAY.

When the American Battle Squadron joined the Grand Fleet in World War I, the Americans had great difficulty in mastering our signals. One day when the whole fleet was at sea a signal to turn was hoisted. When it came down the British ships turned one way, the Americans the other. The U.S.N. Admiral Rodman turned to rend his aide, who forestalled him with "Sorry Admiral, I guess I told you wrong." This has since been quoted as an example of the perfect relationship between Admiral and Flag Lieutenant.

During the operations off Crete in World War II, when cruisers and destroyers which were not sunk were battered and worn out, a flotilla limped into Alexandria. No sooner had they fuelled than they were ordered out again back to Crete. The Rear Admiral commanding Destroyers pointed out to the Commander-in-Chief by signal that his ships were scarcely seaworthy. One of them was leaking badly with one engine out of action and steering defective. Probably one of the toughest signals made during the war was the Commander-in-Chief Mediterranean's reply:

> THIS IS NO TIME FOR DESTROYERS TO BE BREAKING DOWN.

Two Canadian destroyers approached a semi-frozen anchorage.
The first barged her way in through the ice and anchored.

From 1st ship to 2nd ship:

ABIE, ABIE, ABIE MY BOY, WHAT ARE YOU WAITING FOR NOW.

Reply from 2nd ship:

ICEHOLES.

From Flag Officer Greenock to Flag Officer Glasgow:

REGRET QUEEN CHARLOTTE CANNOT WAIT FOR DUCHESS OF
PORTSMOUTH.

A cruiser was trying to secure to head and stern buoys near her
flagship in a congested harbour. The Admiral watched the proceedings from his quarterdeck. The cruiser made a good approach
and appeared to be judging the manœuvre well. The Admiral
signalled:

GOOD.

Then things started to go wrong for the cruiser. She missed
the buoys and got more and more tangled up. After watching
for some time the Admiral again signalled:

ADD TO MY PREVIOUS SIGNAL GOD.

The late Captain F. J. Walker, C.B., D.S.O. and three bars,
showed a quality of skill and leadership which became a legend
in the Atlantic battle against U-boats. His enthusiasm is reflected
in a signal after a fifteen-and-a-half hour hunt which ended in

the sinking of U473, on 5th May, 1944. Shortly after midnight the U-boat surfaced in a desperate effort to escape on her diesel engines. *Starling*, *Wren* and *Wild Goose* pursued her and a running gun battle followed. Finally the U-boat, out of control, circled, and after receiving several direct hits up went her bows and she sank. As she disappeared Captain Walker made his first signal of the action from *Starling*:

CEASE FIRING. GOSH WHAT A LOVELY BATTLE.

On a calm summer's evening a destroyer was steaming down the Minches returning to Londonderry after a convoy conference at Greenock. Suddenly, all chances of a final night in harbour were shattered by this signal from the Admiralty, at top priority:

ENEMY AGENT KNOWN TO HAVE BEEN IN ALDERSHOT RECENTLY SEEN YESTERDAY AT GREENOCK MINGLING WITH TROOPS ABOUT TO EMBARK IN OVERSEAS CONVOY. MOTOR BOAT BELONGING LIGHTHOUSE KEEPER MULL OF KINTYRE REPORTED MISSING AT 0900 TODAY WEDNESDAY. CONSIDER POSSIBLY AGENT HAS STOLEN BOAT AND IS MAKING FOR IRISH FREE STATE WITH IMPORTANT INFORMATION ABOUT CONVOY SAILING TOMORROW. MOTOR SKIFF HULL GREEN, RUBBING STRAKE ORANGE, TANK FULL. MAN 6 FOOT FAIR FRESH COMPLEXION AND LAST SEEN WEARING KHAKI BATTLEDRESS. NO OTHER SHIP AND NO AIRCRAFT AVAILABLE. SEARCH FOR THIS BOAT. REPORT WHEN YOU HAVE FOUND IT.

With less than an hour's daylight left all the destroyer could do was to guess a likely position and steam for it. As she approached the position a speck was sighted. It became a boat, with a man in it. Man and boat answered the description. The boat was hoisted and searched. It contained a copy of *Mein Kampf*, in German. It was like a winner coming home at very long odds. In little more than an hour after the arrival of Admiralty's signal:

From destroyer to Admiralty:

BOAT RECOVERED, MAN ARRESTED.

179

During Russian convoy PQ 16 in May, 1942.
From Ashanti (with convoy) to Admiralty:
NO FURTHER AIR ATTACK TOUCH WOOD. . . . THE SHADOWERS
LIKE THE POOR ARE ALWAYS WITH US.

Farewell message to departing cruiser commanded by a Captain Wright:
PROVERBS 6 V.8.[1]

During World War I an Admiral had invited a friend—Lady A—to lunch the following day. In the morning his Squadron went to sea and he made the following signal to the captain of another ship which was remaining in harbour:
I HAD INVITED LADY A TO LUNCH TODAY BUT AS WE ARE
SAILING UNEXPECTEDLY I WOULD BE GLAD IF YOU WOULD
GIVE HER LUNCHEON INSTEAD. I AM LEAVING MY BARGE
BEHIND WITH ORDERS TO REPORT TO YOU. THIS MAY MAKE IT
EASIER FOR YOU TO LOOK AFTER LADY A. PLEASE MAKE WHAT-
EVER USE OF HER YOU LIKE.

Bombardment of Genoa. H.M.S. *Malaya*, in accordance with tradition flying the Malayan Jack at her Port Yard arm. After the second 15-in. salvo enveloped her in smoke and flame *Malaya* received the following signal from Admiral Somerville in *Renown*:
YOU LOOK LIKE AN ENRAGED P AND O.
(The Malayan Jack and the P. and O. House flag are very similar.)

In reply to a complaint by the master of a Merchant Ship that the route he had been ordered to take was dangerous.
From C.in-C. Med. to Naval Officer in charge, Haifa:
INFORM THE MASTER OF S.S. . . . THAT EVERYWHERE IN THE
MEDITERRANEAN IS DANGEROUS THESE DAYS.

---

[1] "Better is a little with righteousness than great revenues without right."

From submarine (returning from Patrol) to Base:
EXPECT TO ARRIVE 1800 IF FRIENDLY AIRCRAFT WILL STOP
BOMBING ME.

C.-in-C. Eastern Fleet after Fleet Air Arm raid on Sabang:
WE CAUGHT THE NIPS WITH THEIR HEADS DOWN AND THEIR
KIMONOS UP.

A submarine had broken down on surface. Another submarine
had ordered to close her and take her in tow, thereby delaying the
latter's return to harbour considerably. On making contact, the
broken down submarine received:
TAKE MUMMIES HAND.

A battlecruiser arrived in harbour after a long patrol at sea to
receive a signal from her flagship saying that she—the flagship—
was unable to take her turn on patrol, so the returning ship would
have to refuel and put to sea again.

On setting out for the second time the battlecruiser's marine
band were on the quarterdeck, playing a tune which had very
rude words. As she passed as close as possible to the flagship:
From Flagship:
ON LEAVING HARBOUR WHO SELECTS THE BAND TUNES.
The Seagoing ship replied:
NORMALLY THE BANDMASTER BUT ON SPECIAL OCCASIONS THE
CAPTAIN.

From Senior officer to submarine, apparently in difficulties:
WHAT ARE YOU DOING.
From Submarine:
LEARNING A LOT.

Dover Patrol 1918. French destroyers were operating with ours. One afternoon enemy destroyers were sighted by a British and French destroyer who immediately gave chase. The Frenchman kept up for a bit then suddenly dropped astern rapidly in a cloud of smoke and steam.

From French destroyer to British ally:
CAN GO NO MORE. BOILER GO BANG.

*From H*00 *to Y*00*:*
YOO HOO.

From Canadian Training Establishment to Canadian Flag Officer Atlantic:
RENEWAL OF STOCKINGS REQUIRED WHITE WOMANS AND SHOES BLACK WOMANS.

From Rear Admiral Alexandria—General:
PREPARE TO REPEL SEA BORNE ATTACK.
The situation at Alexandria was tense. *Warspite* and *Valiant* had been put out of action in harbour. As dawn broke the local fishing fleet appeared with their sails billowing, making for the harbour entrance after a good night's catch. The signal was soon cancelled but it showed an intelligent appreciation of what the Italians could have done, had they thought of it.

October, 1940. Coastal Command aircraft was laboriously flashing to Cruiser *Dunedin* off Rockall. The ship was returning from Norway.

From Aircraft:

WHAT SHIP.

From Dunedin:

GRAF SPEE.

From Aircraft:

ARE YOU NAVAL TYPES STILL SO FAST ASLEEP THAT YOU HAVEN'T HEARD OF THE END OF THE GRAF SPEE.

From Dunedin:

WHICH END.

One gunboat was being followed up a Chinese river by a second. The first ship rounded a bend and slowed down to wait for the other. As her consort did not appear she called her up by radio.

WHAT IS THE DELAY.

The second gunboat had run aground, and replied:

REGRET HAVE BECOME A SEMI-PERMANENT FEATURE OF THE CHINESE LANDSCAPE.

Cruiser flagship H.M.S. *Trinidad* was attacked repeatedly returning from a Russian convoy. In a further attack by dive-bombers she was set on fire and put out of action. Having regained control the Admiral, for the benefit of the escorting destroyers, hoisted a signal:

I AM PROCEEDING TO THE WESTWARD.

Half an hour later it was decided to abandon ship. Destroyer *Matchless* was ordered to sink her with torpedoes. This signal was still flying when *Trinidad* eventually sank.

From Coastguard Station:
> A SMALL BOAT APPEARS TO BE STATIONARY OFF BROADSTAIRS
> ABOUT ¾ MILE. THE MILITARY HAVE BEEN FIRING AT IT BUT
> GET NO REPLY.

In 1916 a young naval officer was married on board the Flag-ship, H.M.S. *Queen*, at Taranto. Much to his embarrassment and annoyance an Italian officer approached him after the ceremony and kissed him on both cheeks.

In 1941, this naval officer, by then a Rear Admiral, command-ing the Mediterranean aircraft carrier Squadron, met his erstwhile Best Man, another Admiral. The best man reminded the bride-groom that the culprit was now Commander-in-Chief of the Italian Battlefleet.

After the carrier's raid on Taranto the following signals were exchanged:

From ex Best Man:
> CONGRATULATIONS ON PAYING OFF SO WELL A 25 YEAR OLD DEBT.

From ex Bridegroom:
> THANK YOU VERY MUCH, BUT SO FAR ONLY ON ONE CHEEK.

From Captain D, Plymouth to C.-in-C., Nore:
> INTEND PUTTING FISHER GIRL OUT OF ACTION FOR 7 DAYS
> FOR SCRAPING OF BOTTOM.

From Submarine returned from war patrol to flotilla Captain:
> PSALM 17 V. 4.[1]

[1] (Concerning the works of men by the word of thy lips I have kept me from the paths of the destroyers.)

From Admiralty to Admiral Commanding Orkneys and Shetlands:
PYROTECHNICS SIMULATING FLASH OF TRAMWAY TROLLEY BUSES
NOW AVAILABLE FOR CAMOUFLAGE PURPOSES. REPORT NUMBER
REQUIRED.

Reply from Admiral commanding Orkneys and Shetlands:
YOUR . . . NIL. NO TRAMS.

Admiral Lord Charles Beresford, as C.-in-C. Mediterranean,
was flying his flag in H.M.S. *Bulwark*, anchored off Corfu. Some
midshipmen from the flagship were picnicking on a neighbouring
island on which there stood a German convent. As no boat
arrived to collect the midshipmen some of them, who were due
back on board, stripped and swam off to the ship. Some Nuns
from the convent were horrified and reported the matter to the
Kaiser who was in residence at his Palace at Corfu:

From His Imperial Majesty to Commander in Chief:
I AM SORRY TO INFORM YOU THAT THE NUNS ON THE ISLAND
OF . . . HAVE BEEN SHOCKED BY THE ATTIRE OF SOME OF
YOUR YOUNG OFFICERS THIS AFTERNOON.

From C.-in-C. to His Imperial Majesty:
THE INCIDENT IS GREATLY REGRETTED BUT YOUR MAJESTY IS
MISINFORMED ON ONE POINT. THE YOUNG GENTLEMEN IN
QUESTION HAD NO ATTIRE.

From Merchant ship in convoy to escort vessel:

PLEASE CAN YOU LET ME HAVE SOME SORT OF MEDICINE FOR SOME SORT OF RASH.

In World War I H.M.S. *Essex*, patrolling off New York, intercepted on radio a foreign vessel endeavouring to relay a weather forecast. The result was recognisable but unintelligible. When she had finished an American Shore Station cut in with:

NOW TRY THE OTHER FOOT.

H.M. Submarine *Truant*, operating in the Far East at the beginning of the war, experienced distressing conditions of humidity. She included in her subsequent report readings of wet and dry thermometers while diving. This produced the following observation from Flag Officer, Submarines:

From Flag Officer Submarines, to Truant:

THE FIGURES YOU REPORT WILL NOT SUPPORT LIFE.

Convoy ONS5 marked the turning point of affairs between U-boats and escorts in the Battle of the Atlantic. For days the convoy was reported and shadowed. Then in came the U-boat wolf-packs to attack. Each time they ran into the tough ring of escorts and were either sunk or fought off. This was virtually the last appearance of the wolf-packs. On arrival at St. John's, Newfoundland, the signal message was received.

From Prime Minister to Escorts of Convoy ONS5:

MY COMPLIMENTS TO YOU ON YOUR UNCEASING FIGHT WITH THE U-BOATS. PLEASE PASS TO COMMODORE OF THE CONVOY MY ADMIRATION FOR THE STEADINESS OF HIS SHIPS.

From Mid. East to Bombarding Force:

. . . PRISONERS EXCEED 25,000 INCLUDING 2 CORPS COM-MANDERS, 4 DIVISIONAL COMMANDERS, 1 BISHOP ACCOM-PANIED BY 3 NUNS (REPEAT) NUNS.

H.M.S. *Duke of York* was lying alongside Parlatorio wharf, Grand Harbour, Malta, repairing damage resulting from an electrical fire. The work took longer than expected, much to the consternation of all on board who wanted to press on to the Far East and get at the Japs. Finally, on leaving, this signal was made: *1738 25 May/45 From Duke of York to Admiral Superintendent Malta:*

IN ENTERPRISE OF MARTIAL KIND
WHEN THERE IS ANY FIGHTING
WE'D RATHER NOT BE LEFT BEHIND
IT ISN'T SO EXCITING.
BUT WHEN THE FLAMES BEGAN TO LICK
AROUND OUR MULTICORIO
WE VERY NEARLY ENDED UP
THE DUKE OF PARLATORIO.

Scene: Foul Atlantic weather, one destroyer comes across another which has been dismasted.
1st destroyer:
HOW COME.
2nd destroyer:
SCRAPING UNDER VERY LOW CLOUD.

During exercises in peacetime.
From Warspite to destroyer Volunteer:
THANK YOU FOR RECOVERING OUR TORPEDO. ONE VOLUNTEER IS BETTER THAN 10 PRESSED MEN.

Admiral Sir John Fisher signalled to a Captain who was making a mess of a manœuvre:
WHAT THE DEVIL ARE YOU DOING.
The Captain, on his dignity, asked for a repetition of the third word, whereupon the Admiral hoisted:
DEVIL, DEVIL, DEVIL, DEVIL,
on all the yard arm halyards.

From Corvette (returning to base) to Motor Torpedo Boat (setting out on patrol):

GOOD LUCK.

Reply from M.T.B.:

THANKS. ACTUALLY WE RELY ON SKILL.

A Russian convoy, was being steadily shadowed day and night by relays of Blom and Voss flying boats. The aircraft flew round and round the convoy keeping low on the horizon and well out

of range of the escorts' guns. An irritated escort leader told his signalman to make by lamp to the German:

YOU ARE MAKING ME DIZZY, FOR GOD'S SAKE GO ROUND THE OTHER WAY.

The signal was read and acknowledged and the flying boat turned round immediately.

A signal made as H.M.S. *Phoebe* parted company from one command to join another:

ROMANS CHAPTER 16 VERSES 1 AND 2.[1]

[1] "I commend unto you Phebe our sister . . . that ye receive her in the Lord, as becometh Saints, and that ye assist her in whatsoever business she hath need of you; for she hath been a succourer of many, and of myself also."

On 30th June, 1928, the 4th Destroyer Flotilla left the Mediterranean Fleet, then at Navarro, to return to the United Kingdom to Pay Off. The Flotilla steamed between the lines of anchored ships with each ship flying one hoist of *Auld Lang Syne*.

An Admiral, leading a line of carriers, watched one of the destroyer screen trying to cut through the line between his ship and the next astern. The destroyer Captain, anxious not to make the obvious mistake of getting across No. 2's bows, cut too close to the flagship's stern. Sure enough an unlucky roll brought his sea boats' davits in contact with the carrier's stern. The Admiral growled "Make that young blighter a signal." Everyone waited to hear the great man's anger put to words.

From Flag Officer to Destroyer:
IF YOU TOUCH ME THERE AGAIN I SHALL SCREAM.

After the Battle of Matapan.
From Captain of Destroyer Flotilla to C.-in-C. Mediterranean:
HAVE ITALIAN SURVIVORS INCLUDING THE ADMIRAL. HE HAS PILES.
Reply from C.-in-C. Mediterranean:
I AM NOT SURPRISED.

From C.-in-C. Portsmouth to Admiralty, repeated to C.-in-C. Plymouth, C.-in-C. Nore, C.-in-C. Rosyth:
REFERENCE ADMIRALTY MESSAGE . . . A CHAOTIC SITUATION HAS ARISEN. WRENS ARE NOT ALLOWED CLOTHING COUPONS ON THE ASSUMPTION THEY RECEIVE UNIFORMS, BUT THERE IS NO UNIFORM AND OVER 1,000 WRENS IN THE PORTSMOUTH COMMAND ARE STILL IN PLAIN CLOTHES. AT SOME ESTABLISHMENTS NEW ENTRY WRENS ARE NOW WORKING IN BARE LEGS TO SAVE THEIR PAIR OF STOCKINGS FOR WALKING OUT. IN

DUE COURSE A LARGE NUMBER OF WRENS WILL BE WORKING
IN A STATE OF NATURE WHICH ON MANY GROUNDS WOULD
BE UNDESIRABLE. . . .

From C.-in-C. Plymouth to C.-in-C. Portsmouth:
SUGGEST YOU APPLY FOR FIGHTER COVER.

Mediterranean cruisers were practising taking up their escorting
positions on the Royal Yacht. A Frigate was acting as Royal
Yacht. Several senior N.A.T.O. officers were watching the
incident including a French Admiral in the Frigate. The C.-in-C.
intended the occasion to be spectacular. The cruisers turned inwards at 25 knots into line abreast and turned again, passing
about 50 feet either side of the Frigate, who received the full
benefit of their bow-waves.

From Cruiser to Frigate:
WHAT DOES IT FEEL LIKE TO BE THE MEAT IN THE SANDWICH.

From Frigate to Cruiser:
NOT GOOD. NO ROOM FOR THE FRENCH MUSTARD.

From extremely fussy destroyer flotilla captain to destroyer
about to go to sea for exercises:
HOW LONG DO YOU EXPECT TO BE AFTER LEAVING HARBOUR.

From Destroyer:
310 FEET AS USUAL.

From Flag Lieutenant to Senior Officer, Port:
WHO DO YOU RECOMMEND FOR ADMIRAL'S WOMAN.

The Senior officer ashore was most perturbed, he asked for a
repetition of the signal, in due course he received this amendment.

From Flag Lieutenant to Senior Officer, Port:
REFERENCE MY SIGNAL PLEASE INSERT WASHER BETWEEN
ADMIRAL AND WOMAN.

From Flotilla leader to U.S. destroyer who has sunk six Japanese submarines in twelve days:

DAMMIT. HOW DO YOU DO IT.

From destroyer escort:

PERSONNEL AND EQUIPMENT WORKED WITH THE SMOOTHNESS OF WELL OILED CLOCKWORK. AS A RESULT OF OUR EFFORTS RECORDING ANGEL IS WORKING OVERTIME CHECKING IN NIP SUBMARINERS JOINING HONOURABLE ANCESTORS.

From Coastguard Station:

A MINE HAS BEEN WASHED INTO . . . BAY. THERE IS A SMALL BLACK BAND ROUND THE MINE.

At a Spithead Review it was decided that all ships would cheer together. A time table was made out to synchronise the cheering allowing for the distances between ships. At the last moment another ship joined the Fleet and was anchored furthest away from the track of the Royal Yacht. She received the following signal:

From C.-in-C.:

CHEER SHIP 5 SECONDS BEFORE SIGNAL TO CHEER SHIP IS HAULED DOWN.

Admiral conducting bombardment to remainder of Battle Squadron:

WHO KNOCKED THAT LIGHTHOUSE DOWN AND WHY.

From Flagship to private ship:

WHAT ARE YOUR WASH CLOTHES HANGING UP FOR.

Reply from private ship:

SUBMIT TO DRY.

The following signal indicates weather conditions in which Minesweepers worked in North Russia:

2054/26 January. From Captain of 1st Minesweeping Flotilla to Senior Base Naval Officer, North Russia:

REGRET TO REPORT THAT AT 1000/26TH JANUARY HARRIER PASSED THROUGH IOKANKA ENTRANCE BROADSIDE ON WITH BOTH ANCHORS DOWN THEREBY DISREGARDING KOLA INLET GENERAL MEMORANDA NOS. 36 AND 37. THIS PROCEDURE WAS ADOPTED AS THE ONLY ALTERNATIVE TO GROUNDING ON MEDYEJI ISLAND. WHEN SHORTENING IN CABLE IN WIND SOUTH WEST FORCE 10 THE SHIP DRAGGED FASTER THAN THE WINCH COULD HEAVE IN . . . SEAGULL LEFT HARBOUR IN A SIMILAR MANNER. OXLIP LEFT WITHOUT INCIDENT. HYDERABAD WAS REPORTED UNABLE TO PROCEED AND WAS ORDERED TO RETURN TO KOLA INDEPENDENTLY.

From Fleet Air Arm Commander in Carrier to airborne Squadron who are not obeying instructions:

THIS IS MASTER QUOTING HEBREWS CHAPTER 12 VERSE 8. I QUOTE: BUT IF YE BE WITHOUT CHASTISEMENT WHEREOF ALL ARE PARTAKERS THEN ARE YE BASTARDS. UNQUOTE. I SAY AGAIN BASTARDS. OUT.

When the New Zealand Cruiser *Bellona* was preparing to sail for U.K. for the Coronation in 1953, it was decided that as many young ratings as possible should go in her. New Zealand Navy Board made the following signal:

RATINGS DRAFTED TO BELLONA FOR PASSAGE TO UK SHOULD BE VICE TRAINED MEN.

Destroyer *Diamond* had just collided with Cruiser *Swiftsure* during manœuvres at sea. The destroyer was technically in the wrong. When they had sorted themselves out:

From Swiftsure to Diamond:

WHAT DO YOU INTEND TO DO NOW.

From Diamond to Swiftsure:

BUY A FARM.

Operation COAT was the codeword given to the passage of a reinforcement from Force H, at one end of the Mediterranean to the Mediterranean Fleet at the other end. The force was late, and only arrived one day before the already planned attack on Taranto.

From C.-in-C. Mediterranean to Flag Officer Force H:

THANK YOU FOR MY COAT. I NEARLY CAUGHT A COLD WAITING FOR IT. I STILL HAVE NO TROUSERS BUT INTEND TAKING THOSE OFF MUSSOLINI SHORTLY.

H.M.S. *Queen Elizabeth* and Cunard liner *Queen Elizabeth* met for the first time in mid-Atlantic.

Queen Elizabeth to Queen Elizabeth:

SNAP.

Two frigates approaching Portland Harbour in channel gale, visibility nil.

From 1st Frigate:

WHEN DO YOU EXPECT TO SIGHT PORTLAND BREAKWATER.

Reply:
> FIFTEEN MINUTES AGO. ESTIMATE MY POSITION 4TH FAIRWAY, CAME GOLF COURSE.

From personal friend of Imperious Admiral who had recently fallen from his barge into the sea.
> I AM SURPRISED THAT A MAN OF YOUR EXPERIENCE SHOULD ATTEMPT TO DO WHAT ONLY ONE MAN HAS DONE BEFORE—WALK ASHORE.

From Captain of 2nd Destroyer Flotilla in 1940 when his flotilla, while trying to draw the enemy, were being chased by two Italian cruisers.
Hyperion to Destroyers in company:
> DON'T LOOK ROUND NOW BUT I THINK WE ARE BEING FOLLOWED.

Scene: Admiral's bridge of H.M.S. *Nelson* with King George VI on board. The fleet was approaching the anchorage in Weymouth Bay. The speed of the fleet was being reduced to 6 knots before anchoring. The signal for speed in those days was letter G. The following was heard:
Signal Officer to Flag Deck "George 6 Hoist."
Signal Officer to Flag Deck "George 6—execute."
His Majesty is said to have flinched, but he made no comment.

From *Formidable*, after being attacked by *Kamikaze*, to *Indomitable* (flying flag of Admiral Vian):
> LITTLE YELLOW BASTARD.
Reply from *Indomitable*:
> ARE YOU REFERRING TO ME.

Early in May, 1943, enemy resistance in Tunisia was collapsing. British naval forces were disposed to prevent any large scale withdrawal of the enemy by sea from the Cape Bon area. He was to be given no chance of staging a Dunkirk evacuation.

1251 8th May. *From C.-in-C. Mediterranean to Destroyers on patrol —Laforey, Bicester, Aldenham, Jervis:*

SINK, BURN AND DESTROY. LET NOTHING PASS.

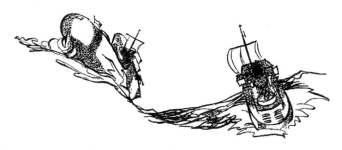

From one corvette to another in full Atlantic gale:

HAVE JUST SEEN DOWN YOUR FUNNEL. FIRE IS BURNING BRIGHTLY.

Before World War I, the combined Mediterranean and Channel Fleets were lying at Lagos. The following general signal was sent by the flagship:

HIS MAJESTY THE KING OF PORTUGAL HAS KINDLY PRESENTED SEVEN TINS OF TUNNY FISH TO EACH SHIP. BOATS ARE TO BE SENT TO COLLECT AT 1600.

Only one ship sent a launch capable of carrying seven tons.

From Local Naval Base to destroyer which has grounded in vicinity:

REQUEST YOU WILL CONSIDER YOURSELVES HONORARY MEMBERS DURING YOUR STAY.

Two ships wishing to exchange movie films:
WILL BE GLAD TO EXCHANGE FANNY BY GASLIGHT FOR TWIN BEDS.

Signal made on conclusion of a Mediterranean operation.
From Flag Officer Force H to C.-in-C. Mediterranean:
. . . ABSENCE OF AIR OPPOSITION LEADS ME TO SUSPECT THAT
NEIGHBOURING TENANT IS FEEDING MY BIRDS.

Between two Atlantic convoy escorts:
1st ship:
COMMENCE HOSTILITIES WITH JAPAN.
2nd ship:
REQUEST PERMISSION TO FINISH BREAKFAST FIRST.

There was no particular signal to initiate the Normandy
Landing. The huge operation ran to a time table, with each
Assault Force operating independently, once D day had been
established. The initiation was metaphorically a nod from the
meteorologists.

On the other hand, once the operation started there must have
been many signals, of which the following is typical. The first
groups of landing craft from the Portsmouth area sailed at 0900,
5th June. As the first convoy left Spithead the signal:
GOOD LUCK. DRIVE ON.
was hoisted in *Largs* (Admiral Talbot's flagship) anchored at the
Eastern end of the lines of landing craft. It remained flying until
Largs got under way at 2145.

Extract from a signal from Senior Naval Officer Archangel to
Senior Naval Officer North Russia:
. . . HE IS A TALKATIVE MAN AND IS ALLEGED TO HAVE TOLD
RADIO OFFICER MOFFAT OF EMPIRE BARD THAT HE RETURNED
LAST NIGHT TO FIND TWO DANES IN BED WITH HIS WIFE AND
THAT HE SHOT THEM BOTH. CONSEQUENTLY HE WOULD DO
ANYTHING TO BE ALLOWED TO RETURN TO U.K.

From Flagship to Cruiser which is out of station:
WHAT ARE YOU DOING.
From Cruiser:
20 KNOTS.

Scene: Spithead Review. Beautiful summer afternoon. Hundreds of yachts sailing between lines of anchored ships. A yacht sailed by a particularly beautiful girl is closely observed by Admiral and Flag Lieutenant from quarter deck of cruiser flagship. Admiral instructs Flag Lieutenant to make a suitable flag signal to the yacht in international code. Flag Lieutenant thumbs through vocabulary and instructs flag deck to hoist three flag signal: D-I-N, which means:
I WILL KEEP CLOSE TO YOU DURING THE NIGHT.
Signal is acknowledged by yacht. Through powerful glasses girl's shoulders observed heaving but whether from laughter or suppressed indignation will never be known by Admiral.

From Royal Yacht off Cowes to H.M.S. *Bittern,* one of the first small ships fitted with stabilisers:
WILL YOU PLEASE ROLL YOUR SHIP FOR HER MAJESTY.

Reply to signal received by an officer, congratulating him on his promotion:
VMT. PSALM 140, 2ND HALF OF VERSE 5.[1]

H.M.S. *Southampton,* cruiser flagship, had the ship's name designed in an unusually dazzling plaque. In harbour one evening when this plaque was illuminated she received the following signal from a senior admiral:
AS A SHAREHOLDER IN THE SOUTHERN RAILWAY I MUST PROTEST ON WHAT CAN ONLY BE CALLED PILFERING ON THE PART OF YOUR FLAGSHIP OF ONE OF THE PLATFORM SIGNS OF THE STATION WHOSE NAME YOU BEAR.

[1] "They have set gins for me."

One night a corvette chased a U-boat away from a convoy and attacked it. The attack was successful, the U-boat surfaced and her crew started to abandon ship. For a few moments the Scottish captain observed the scene lost in admiration of his achievement. Then he "came to" and realised the gap between him and the convoy was widening rapidly. He also remembered that picking up U-boat survivors was secondary to guarding the convoy. Shining his Aldis Signal lamp in an Easterly direction therefore he steamed past the U-boat, and to ease his conscience he said through the loud hailer:

MY LIGHT IS SHINING ROUGHLY IN THE DIRECTION OF GERMANY —GOOD NIGHT.

REQUEST THE PLEASURE OF THE COMPANY OF ADMIRAL AND MRS . . . AT DINNER TONIGHT 1930.

Reply:

VERY MANY THANKS. ADMIRAL AND MRS . . . HAVE A DAUGHTER.

Reply:

QUITE UNDERSTAND. HEARTIEST CONGRATULATIONS.

From Flag Officer Eastern Fleet—General:

0831/24/12/1943. EVERYBODY WISHES EVERYBODY ELSE A VERY HAPPY CHRISTMAS AND NEW YEAR. NO FURTHER SIGNALS ARE TO BE MADE. THINK OF THE SIGNALMEN AND THE PAPER SHORTAGE.

From permanently irritated Admiral, to Cruiser Flagship lying alongside (whose Admiral he took to be ashore):

I OBSERVE MEN ON YOUR UPPER DECK WHO ARE NOT IN THE CORRECT RIG OF THE DAY.

From Senior Cruiser Admiral, who was in fact on board:

I OBSERVE THAT YOU OBSERVE TOO MUCH.

From Commander-in-Chief, Western Approaches to the
Senior Officer of a special flotilla formed for training our Escort
Groups in the Atlantic:

THE TRYING CONDITIONS OF A FULL GALE ON SATURDAY
NIGHT AND EASTER SUNDAY MORNING MIGHT WELL HAVE
PERSUADED A LESS RESOLUTE TEAM THAN YOURS TO HAVE
ABANDONED THE EXERCISES FOR SHELTER.

From Admiralty:

IT HAS BEEN DECIDED TO DISCONTINUE USE OF BALLOONS IN
ALL THEATRES WITH POSSIBLE EXCEPTION OF FAR EAST.

In winter, 1940, when Wrens were buying up all available serge to
make trousers, a Commander-in-Chief made the following signal:

WRENS CLOTHING IS TO BE HELD UP UNTIL THE NEEDS OF
SEAGOING PERSONNEL HAVE BEEN SATISFIED.

27th April, 1941. From Athens wireless station (as Germans
entered Athens):

CLOSING DOWN FOR THE LAST TIME HOPING FOR HAPPIER
DAYS. GOD BE WITH YOU AND FOR YOU.

then . . . silence.

An American destroyer new to our Signal methods was seen in the Atlantic flying two flags: Church Pennant and Interrogative Flag. On being asked what the signal was intended to mean she replied:

GOD, WHERE AM I.

Eastern Fleet, returned from sea, "hove to" outside Trincomalee waiting to proceed one by one up the swept channel to the anchorage. Apart from ships being vulnerable to torpedo attack everyone was short of sleep and touchy. Suddenly an American Merchant ship appeared and, ploughing through the waiting ships, shaped up for the swept channel. The tricky situation was relieved by Admiral Sir James Somerville's ability to sum anyone up quickly:

C.-in-C. to U.S. Merchant ship:

AS MAE WEST SAYS, ONE AT A TIME BOYS.

The Bombardment of Genoa on 9th February, 1941, by Force H was followed by 48 hours' wireless silence. Then from Flag Officer Force H to Admiralty:

BOMBARDMENT COMPLETED. (Pause.) FROM ALL ACCOUNTS GENOA IS IN A BLOODY FINE MESS.

This was followed by a further silence of 48 hours.

The famous brothers, Admirals Howard and Joe Kelly, rarely demonstrated their affection for one another. These signals followed the grounding of Admiral Howard Kelly's yacht, when he was Commander-in-Chief, China Station between the wars.

From J. to H.:

GLAD YOU'RE SAVED.

From H. to J.:

GLAD YOU'RE GLAD.

From Base to ship:
1st version:
    HAVE (blank) WOMEN FOR YOU.
Correction:
    HAVE TWO MEN FOR YOU.

From small South Korean craft to British Patrol vessel:
    WE PUT TO PATROL AT 2000. THE SEA IS BAD. MY SHIP SHE IS
    LIKE RAGS AND I HAVE NO CONFIDENCE IN HIM THIS WEATHER.
    I BEG WITH PARDON YOU MUST TELL ME PUT ASHORE.

In 1940 submarine *Sealion*, after attacking a convoy in the
Skaggerak was rammed and heavily depth-charged. When she
eventually surfaced she was a shambles. No periscopes, no wireless,
but still alive. As she was surrounded by enemy D/F stations any
signal she sent would have to be short. Eventually the wireless
was repaired and the following signal transmitted:
From Sealion to Flag Officer Submarines:
    SEALION RAMMED AND RETURNING TO BASE. BLIND BUT
    BLYTH.
The last word was signalled as the place name but it was
understood.

From Bairoko (American ship) to H.M.S. Cossack:
    SHIPS BEING ACCEPTED BY HELO WILL KEEP CLEAR OF FANTAIL
    CRANE AFTER MOUNT FORWARD AND DEPRESS AND SEND CREW
    INDEPENDENTLY TO PLACE WIND 30 DEGREES ON STARBOARD
    BOW.
or, in other words
    WHEN HELICOPTER ARRIVES, QUARTERDECK IS TO BE CLEARED
    AND Y TURRET TRAINED FORWARD AND GUNS DEPRESSED.
    SHIP IS TO ACT INDEPENDENTLY TO PLACE WIND 30 DEGREES
    ON STARBOARD BOW.

On her maiden voyage to Malta the paint peeled in a distressing manner from the sides of H.M. Yacht *Britannia*. The captain reported the matter in detail to the Commander-in-Chief, Mediterranean, on 20th April, 1954, concluding his signal as follows:

. . . PEELING HAS EVEN OCCURRED RIGHT UP MY STERN.

From Commander-in-Chief, Mediterranean:

I AM MUCH RELIEVED TO FIND THAT IT IS YOUR SHIP AND NOT YOU WHO WILL BE UNFIT FOR POLO.

From Vice Admiral Dover to C.-in-C. Nore:

THE SERVICES OF LADY BRASSEY LAST NIGHT IN WHAT MIGHT HAVE BEEN A DIFFICULT PREDICAMENT WERE MUCH APPRECIATED, PARTICULARLY BY WAR NIZAM.

A carrier was flying on aircraft which necessitated her steaming head to wind. By the Rules of the Road she should have given way to an approaching cruiser flagship but she remained on her course. The cruiser passed very close indeed astern of the carrier.

Cruiser Flagship to Carrier:

LUCKY THE TAIL OF YOUR SHIRT WAS NOT HANGING OUT.

During the Munich crisis a destroyer and a submarine were carrying out exercises together off Gibraltar. On return to harbour a large and heavy-laden German freighter passed nearby.

From Submarine to Destroyer:

REQUEST PERMISSION TO START THE WAR.

Sailors have their own views about the pronunciation of ships' names. *Penelope*, for example, is usually known as Pennyloap. When she met destroyer *Antelope* at sea, the following signal was made:

From Penelope to Antelope:

AT LONG LAST ANTELLYPEE MEETS PENNYLOAP.

Two signals, separated by 7½ hours, made by H.M.S. *Amethyst* at the start and finish of her perilous run down the Yangtse River past Communist forts and shore batteries.

From Amethyst to C.-in-C.:

AM UNDER WAY AND UNDER HEAVY FIRE FROM SHORE BATTERIES.

From Amethyst to C.-in-C.:

HAVE REJOINED THE FLEET SOUTH OF WOOSUNG. NO DAMAGE OR CASUALTIES. GOD SAVE THE KING.

Ex-Corvette *Coreopsis*, hired by Ealing Studios for making the film "The Cruel Sea," entered Portland Harbour after a day's "shooting." She was meant to look as if she had been battered about in Atlantic weather, and she did. Her white ensign was being exchanged for a red one as she passed U.S.S. *Missouri*, "the Mighty Mo," berthed in Portland Harbour:

From U.S.S. Missouri to Coreopsis:

WHAT SHIP.

From M.V. Coreopsis:

H.M.S. COMPASS ROSE SAILING THE CRUEL SEA (pause) WHAT SHIP.

No reply.

A ship was carrying out low level A.A. practice at a drogue target supposed to be at 2,000 feet. The pilot of the plane obviously had not read the orders for the exercise, and for an hour he flew up and down over the ship at 5,000 feet. Finally the pilot signalled to the ship:

I AM AT 5000 FEET. SHALL I COME DOWN.

The ship replied:

I THINK IT WOULD BE QUICKER IF I CAME UP TO YOU.

From Captain Walker to his famous Atlantic Escort Group, when he had come to the conclusion that the particular underwater Asdic contact they were investigating was not a U-boat:

I AM AFRAID WE MUST LEAVE AND PUT IT DOWN TO AN ICHTHYOLOGICAL GEFUFFLE.

Time 0700. Squadron at sea, having sailed the previous midnight from port at which the entertainment had been lavish:

From ship to Flagship:

SUBMIT, GOOD MORNING.

From Flagship:

NOT APPROVED. THE MATTER WILL BE RECONSIDERED AFTER BREAKFAST.

Concluding remarks by Flag Officer Force H to signal report of Malta convoy operation on 25th July, 1941:

I HAVE RESTORED GOOD CONDUCT BADGE TO FORCE H GUARDIAN ANGEL, DEPRIVED FOR OFFENCES COMMITTED ON DAY I AND DAY 3.

Extract from a signalled report on operation STYLE, 4th August, 1941.

. . . FAILURE OF ENEMY TO DEAL WITH FORCES ENGAGED ATTRIBUTED TO PREVIOUS ROUGH HANDLING OF SURFACE

FORCES BY MEDITERRANEAN FLEET AND SUCCESSFUL OPERA-
TIONS OF OUR SUBMARINES. ENEMY IN FACT APPEARED TO
HAVE BEEN COMPLETELY BOTCHED, BEGGARED AND BEWIL-
DERED.

From American destroyer to Flag Officer Queenstown:
HAVE ATTACKED AND SUNK ENEMY SUBMARINE. WHERE AM I.
From Flag Officer Queenstown:
TOP OF THE CLASS.

Two destroyers home from abroad securing alongside dock-
yard jetty. Both ships have been friendly rivals throughout
commission on foreign station.
From 1st Destroyer to 2nd Destroyer:
IF THE BEARDED CAPTAIN WILL GET IN TOUCH WITH THE LADY
ON THE JETTY PUSHING THE PRAM HE WILL LEARN SOMETHING
WHICH WILL TAKE THAT GRIN OFF HIS FACE.

From Vice Admiral (Air) to Glorious:
I PROPOSE INCORPORATING THE FOLLOWING IN MY LETTER OF
PROCEEDINGS, HEARD ON R/T FROM GLADIATORS PATROL THIS
AFTERNOON—TALLY HO TALLY HO I SEE THE BASTARDS. THIS
ALLEGATION ON THE PARENTAGE OF THE CREW OF THE JUNKERS
87 ATTACKED WAS PROVED TO BE UNFOUNDED WHEN THEY
WERE SUBSEQUENTLY RESCUED.

On an occasion when Fleets were being mobilised some Royal
Marine Bandsmen got all mixed up due to an error in drafting.
One ship made a general signal·
I CAN OFFER 2 PICCOLOS AND A BASSOON IN EXCHANGE FOR
3 TROMBONES AND A BIG DRUM.

Narvik, the railhead of the Norwegian iron ore industry, was in German hands.

To the north of the town the railway follows the coast and enters a tunnel about ¼ mile long.

Two destroyers were patrolling in the vicinity one sunny morning in May 1940. Destroyer B received the following signal from A:

> ORDERS FOR OPERATION LETS PLAY TRAINS. THE 11.30 FROM NARVIK IS ALMOST DUE. DESTROYER A WILL TAKE STATION TO SOUTHWARD AND HASTEN TRAIN INTO TUNNEL WITH H.E. AFTER 2ND SALVO DESTROYER B IS TO COMMENCE GREETING TRAIN IN SIMILAR MANNER AT NORTHERN END OF TUNNEL.

From dissatisfied Admiral during manoeuvres to private ship:
> WOULD IT NOT HAVE BEEN BETTER TO HAVE TURNED TO STARBOARD.

Reply:
> YES.

Two Mediterranean destroyers being attacked periodically by enemy aircraft.

From 1st Destroyer:
> TODAY IS CORONATION DAY.

Reply from 2nd Destroyer:
> HOPE YOU DON'T GET CROWNED.

A classic understatement when *Illustrious* rejoined the Mediterranean Fleet the morning after the brilliant Fleet Air Arm raid on Taranto.

From Commander-in-Chief to Illustrious:
MANOEUVRE WELL EXECUTED.

From C.-in-C. Mediterranean to Vice Admiral, Malta:
DRIVE A LONG HAT PIN INTO THE STERN OF THE OFFICER RESPONSIBLE FOR REPORTING MERCHANT SHIPPING MOVEMENTS.

The Senior Officer of a Motor Torpedo Boat Flotilla, operating from a temporary base, had quarters in the local hotel. He returned one night late from London to find his room was occupied. Next day he sent the following signal to the flotilla:
OFFICERS ARE REMINDED THAT THE S.O.'S CABIN IS NOT REPEAT NOT TO BE USED FOR PURPOSES OTHER THAN THOSE LAID DOWN IN THE BOY SCOUT MANUAL.

In July, 1943, a minesweeper entered Syracuse harbour towing a captured Italian submarine. She looked very pleased with herself. Another minesweeper leaving harbour signalled:
IS THAT YOUR FIRST TODAY.

On a Russian convoy in May, 1942, U.S.S.R. gunboat collided with H.M.S. *Harrier*. Later the following signal was sent:
From Rubin to Harrier:
I AM VERY SORRY WHAT INJURED YOUR SHIP BY APPROACH TO BOARD FOR WHAT I MUST TO BEG PARDON. WE ARE PROUD OF STAUNCHNESS AND COURAGE ENGLISH SEAMENS OUR ALLIES.

To add to the strain of the operations off Crete, there was an abundance of signalling. Everyone from Admirals downwards signalled their day and night intentions. At dusk one destroyer, fed up with reading all these signals, grumbled to another ship:
THE ROAD TO CRETE IS PAVED WITH NIGHT INTENTIONS.

Destroyer reporting having to leave refugees without any food:

... THEY REMAIN SANS BEURRE ET SANS BRIOCHES.

From C.-in-C. Mediterranean to Sunderland aircraft which has just announced proudly by signal that she has shot down a small Italian shadower.

YOU GREAT BIG BULLY.

When the Australian Cruiser *Brisbane* was visiting Hongkong the flagship of the China Fleet, H.M.S. *Hawkins*, gave an "At home" to enable the officers of the *Brisbane* to meet the local ladies. Whilst this At home was in progress a swarm of bees settled on the quarterdeck awning of the *Brisbane*. The Officer of the watch in the *Hawkins*, observing this phenomenon through his telescope immediately made a signal to the *Brisbane*:

HOW MANY BEES IN BRISBANE.

Back came the reply from the Australian Officer of the watch:

HOW MANY HAWS IN HAWKINS.

From Corvette to Base:

AM TIED UP TO NO. 5 BERTH.

From Base:

SHOE LACES ARE TIED UP. H.M. SHIPS ARE SECURED.

In a Mediterranean convoy operation *Nelson*, flying the flag of Flag Officer Force H, was torpedoed.

From C.-in-C. Mediterranean to Flag Officer Force H:

I HOPE THAT THESE MY CONGRATULATIONS WILL COMPENSATE FOR A SLAP IN THE BELLY WITH A WET FISH.

From Flag Officer Force H to C.-in-C. Mediterranean:

THANK YOU. AT MY AGE KICKS BELOW THE BELT HAVE LITTLE SIGNIFICANCE.

H.M. Minesweepers *Prompt* and *Jason* were built, launched, commissioned and operated together. They were chummy ships and much friendly rivalry existed between them. One day *Prompt* struck an acoustic mine. While she was settling down in the water with upper deck awash:

From Prompt to Jason:

FIRST AGAIN.

The Flagship was refitting. The remainder of the Battle Cruiser Squadron were being led up to the anchorage by the next Senior Captain who had not had much experience in handling the Squadron. The signal to stop engines was hoisted. When it was hauled down the leading ship did not stop her own engines, and soon began to draw away from the others.

From next astern to Leading ship:

WHAT SPEED ARE YOU STOPPED AT PLEASE.

From Senior Base Naval Officer, North Russia to Senior Officer, Force R (visiting):

THE RUSSIAN ADMIRAL HAS SENT TO MY OFFICE A PRESENT TO BE FORWARDED TO YOU BUT I REGRET VERY MUCH THAT THE CUSTOMS FORMALITIES IMPOSED ON ME BY OUR BRAVE ALLIES PREVENTS ME FROM SENDING IT TO YOU UNTIL PASSED FOR EXPORT. IT IS ALSO MOST UNFORTUNATE THAT I HAVE FELT COMPELLED TO WITHHOLD FROM HIM THE PRESENT THAT C.-IN-C. HOME FLEET SENT HIM UNTIL OUR GLORIOUS ALLIES ALLOW ME TO RECEIVE OUR OWN PRIVATE MAIL WHICH YOU BROUGHT OUT. THE ADMIRAL HAS BEEN INFORMED IN EACH CASE. PLEASE EXPLAIN TO COMMANDER IN CHIEF.

From Admiral to Ship:

WHILST AFLOAT WITH MY FLAG FLYING I PASSED YOUR SHIP AT 1250. IT REMINDED ME OF AN AVIARY WITH THE SHIP'S COMPANY SITTING ON THE RAILS WITH TAILS TOWARDS ME LIKE BIRDS ON A TWIG.

In the Mediterranean a submarine was ordered to try out a new route through a supposed enemy minefield, which entailed an all day dive in thickly mined waters. It was a grim form of trial and error, but it was the only way of finding a channel through which our submarines could pass. The result of the experiment, as received by the Captain of the submarine flotilla at Malta was:

From Submarine Urchin:

NEXT PLEASE.

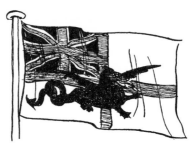

The Flag of the Zeebrugge Association is derived from the following signals.

From Warwick (destroyer flying the flag of Rear Admiral Roger Keyes leading force to attack Zeebrugge on eve of St. George's Day 1918):

ST. GEORGE FOR ENGLAND.

From Vindictive (Captain Carpenter, shortly to win V.C.):

MAY WE GIVE THE DRAGON'S TAIL A DAMNED GOOD TWIST.

A Corvette was passing the Barr light vessel off Liverpool when she touched off a magnetic mine somewhere in the shallows. It did not do much damage beyond bending the main shaft. A signal was sent by the Corvette to the Port War Signal Station reporting the incident.

From Commander-in-Chief Western Approaches came the somewhat heartless reply:

DO NOT SINK IN THE SWEPT CHANNEL.

SCRAP LOG

From Cruiser to Admiral:

MY SEAPLANE IS OUT OF ACTION DUE TO SEAGULLS STROPPING THEIR BEAKS ON FABRIC.

From 1st Cruiser to 2nd Cruiser (in harbour at anchor):

YOUR MOTORBOAT HAS JUST DESTROYED MY STARBOARD GANGWAY. IT SEEMS THAT YOUR COXSWAIN COMPLETELY LOST HIS HEAD.

Reply:

PLEASE SEND BACK MY COXSWAIN'S HEAD.

22nd December, 1854, Crimean War. Vice Admiral James Dundas was turning over to Rear Admiral Sir Edmund Lyons. The relationship of these two officers is revealed in their parting signals:

From Britannia (Admiral Dundas) to Agamemnon (Admiral Lyons):

MAY SUCCESS ATTEND YOU.

Reply from Agamemnon:

MAY HANGING AWAIT YOU.

From Renown:

AM BEING ATTACKED BY ELEVEN DIVE-BOMBERS.

Later:

SEVEN DIVE-BOMBERS WILL NOT BAT IN SECOND INNINGS.

Signal being received:

. . . THE FLEET WILL ACT AS A HOLE IN A BAYONET (pause).

Correction:

THE FLEET WILL ACT AS A WHOLE IN OBEYING IT.

Winter afternoon, 1940. Four destroyers approaching Scottish coast from the Atlantic. Filthy weather. Low cloud, low visibility. No means of knowing their exact position.
From Kipling to Kelly:

> ATTENTION IS INVITED TO THE TEMPEST ACT I SCENE I LAST 4 LINES.[1]

1914–18 War. *Cyclamen to V.A. Malta* (after sinking Allied Italian Submarine mistaken for U-boat):

> HAVE RAMMED AND SUNK ENEMY SUBMARINE. SURVIVORS APPEAR TO SPEAK ITALIAN.

From Cruiser entering harbour to Base:

> HAVE YOU ANY NEWS OF LADY BLANCHE.

From Base:

> HAS LADY IN QUESTION LEGS OR PROPELLORS.

Destroyer *Virago* was in collision with *Emperor* while transferring stores at sea.
From Captain of Flotilla:

> IN SPITE OF YOUR NAME YOU MUST GET OUT OF THE HABIT OF SNAPPING AT THESE GREAT BIG MEN.

A severe air raid at Algiers coincided with a Fourth of June Etonian Dinner. Subsequently a question was asked in the House of Commons as to whether service fireworks had been used at public expense for an Old Etonian celebration. The following is an extract of Commander-in-Chief Mediterranean's signal on the matter.

---

[1] "Now would I give a thousand furlongs of sea for an acre of barren ground—long heath, broom, furze, any thing. The wills above be done! but I would fain die a dry death."

. . . THE ONLY INCIDENT BEARING ON THIS SUBJECT IS THAT DURING A 4TH JUNE OLD ETONIAN DINNER AT ALGIERS AN AIR RAID TOOK PLACE ON THE PORT. DURING THIS RAID THOSE DINING WERE TREATED TO A SPECTACULAR ROCKET DISPLAY WHEN THE PROJECTORS WERE FIRED, AN OFFICER BEING HEARD TO REMARK IN APPRECIATIVE TONES ON THE FIREWORK DISPLAY SO KINDLY ARRANGED FOR THEIR FESTIVAL BY THE NAVY. IT IS REGRETTED THAT THE EXIGENCIES OF WAR SHOULD HAVE GIVEN COLOUR TO THE IDEA THAT GOVERNMENT SUPPORT WAS BEING GIVEN TO THE ACTIVITIES OF THIS NEFARIOUS SECT. SHOULD IT BE CONSIDERED OF SUFFICIENT IMPORTANCE TO JUSTIFY THE WASTE OF TIME AND EFFORT I CAN OF COURSE CONTINUE MY ENQUIRIES THROUGH ALL THE PORTS IN NORTH AFRICA, IN WHICH CASE PERHAPS THE HON. MEMBER WILL FURNISH MORE DETAILS. I AM HOWEVER OF THE OPINION THAT THIS IS THE BASIS OF THE STORY, AND THAT THE HON. MEMBER'S INFORMANT MUST ALSO HAVE BEEN CELEBRATING.

Ships assembled to greet Her Majesty about to pass in Royal Yacht. One ship is in doubt as to how many "hips" should precede "Hooray" when giving three cheers.

1st Ship to 2nd Ship:

INTERROGATIVE 2 HIPS OR 3.

Reply:

2 AS IN MARILYN MONROE.

From Commander-in-Chief—General:

DRESS FOR COMMANDER-IN-CHIEF'S PICNIC TOMORROW SUN-DAY, PLAIN CLOTHES. THIS DOES NOT INCLUDE MIDSHIPMAN . . .'S YELLOW PLUS FOURS.

Gibraltar Signal Station to passing ship:

WHAT SHIP?

Reply:

WHAT ROCK?

H.M.S. *Shah*, escort carrier, built in Vancouver, was entering San Francisco on her maiden voyage down the West Coast.

From San Francisco Port War Signal Station to Shah:

WHAT SHIP.

From Shah:

HMSSHAH.

Port War Signal Station:

REPEAT.

After several repeats:

NEVER MIND WE WILL FIND OUT WHEN YOU GET IN.

Flotilla of Canadian Motor Launches in line ahead. Fog descends, fog buoys are streamed. Fog lifts completely, all fog buoys are recovered except one, whose owner has apparently forgotten its existence.

From M.L. following to owner of fog buoy:

TELL THE CAPTAIN THERE'S NO BEER LEFT IN THIS KEG.

From Cruiser relieving Malta:

WE ARE DELIVERING THE MILK. ANY EMPTIES TO COLLECT.

Reply:

YES, 26 GERMAN AND ITALIAN PRISONERS OF WAR.

Two submarines were accompanying a Russian convoy. One submarine Captain thought it would be a good idea to show himself if the convoy was attacked. He therefore made a signal to the Senior Officer of the escort.

IN THE EVENT OF ATTACK BY HEAVY SURFACE FORCES, INTEND TO REMAIN ON THE SURFACE.

The destroyer Escort Commander replied immediately:

SO DO I.

From Commander-in-Chief Mediterranean, Admiral Cunningham to Admiral Commanding Force H, Admiral Somerville, already a K.B.E., on the occasion of his receiving the K.C.B.

> FANCY, TWICE A KNIGHT AND AT YOUR AGE. CONGRATULATIONS.

From St. Helena to Bermuda:

> ASCENSION ADVISES THREE DENTURES FOUND IN CAR AFTER CRICKET SUNDAY, 7 DECEMBER. DO THEY BELONG TO YOU PLEASE, IF SO INDICATE DISPOSAL.

From Bermuda to St. Helena:

> ARE TEETH MARKED WITH BROAD ARROWS.

From Cruiser to destroyer who is acting as a Merchant ship in a trade defence exercise, and has been captured.

> HAVE YOU ANY WOMEN ON BOARD.

From Destroyer:

> NO, THEY HAVE ALL BEEN SHOT. THEY PREFERRED DEATH TO DISHONOUR.

Manœuvres were being carried out by destroyers conducted by a Cruiser flagship. They finished up with the somewhat hair-raising V.I.P. escort manœuvre, in which two divisions of destroyers approached the V.I.P. (Cruiser) on opposite courses, turning inwards to form a close escort. One destroyer misjudged the distance and finished by passing much too close to the V.I.P.

From Admiral to Destroyer:

> THE EMPEROR WAS MUCH IMPRESSED BY THAT MANOEUVRE BUT NOT SO THE BRITISH NAVAL ATTACHE WHO HAS GONE BELOW TO CHANGE HIS TROUSERS.

Admiral Sir James Somerville on first sighting his Eastern Fleet off Ceylon, observed a mixed party with hardly any two ships of the same class present.

C.-in-C. Eastern Fleet to Eastern Fleet:

SO THIS IS THE EASTERN FLEET. WELL NEVER MIND. THERE'S MANY A GOOD TUNE PLAYED ON AN OLD FIDDLE.

One Canadian destroyer overtaking another in race for home:

PARDON ME BUT YOUR SHIP IS SLOWING.

From Senior Ship to Junior Ship:

YOUR JACK IS UPSIDE DOWN.

From Junior Ship:

THIS IS HOW IT WAS RECEIVED FROM NAVAL STORE OFFICER PORTSMOUTH.

From Senior Ship:

SOME PEOPLE WOULD DRINK SULPHURIC ACID IF IT CAME IN A GIN BOTTLE.

Dark night, North Sea.

From Destroyer A to Admiralty:

HAVE BEEN HIT RIGHT AFT BY MINE.

From Destroyer B to Admiralty:

REFERENCE DESTROYER A'S SIGNAL. NOT MINE BUT ME.

When H.M.S. *Valiant*, newly refitted battleship, was exchanged from the Western Mediterranean for H.M.S. *Malaya*, the latter suffered from condenser and other troubles. C.-in-C. Med. made a polite "thank you" signal to Flag Officer Force H, hoping *Malaya* would serve him well. The reply from Flag Officer Force H was carefully coded up as follows:

THOUGH NOT WISHING TO LOOK A GIFT HORSE IN THE MOUTH, I UNDERSTAND THAT THIS (THREE CORRUPT GROUPS) HAS TROUBLE WITH HER TUBES.

From Cotswold:
BELGIA BOMBED BY SUNK LIGHT VESSEL

From 1st Destroyer to 2nd Destroyer:
MY PORT SHAFT IS RUNNING HOT.
From 2nd Destroyer to 1st Destroyer:
AS THE SEWING MACHINE SAID IN THE NUDIST CAMP, SO WHAT.

A convoy escort developed a defect which necessitated her limping home from her mid-Atlantic charges. There was a thick fog as she lay close to the senior officer's ship receiving her instructions.
From S.O. to Escort:
. . . HOPE YOU FIND NECESSARY FACILITIES IN BELFAST.
From Escort to S.O.:
HOPE I FIND BELFAST.

After the Battle of Jutland:
JOIN ME. WHERE AM I.

217

From Boom Defence Officer to C.-in-C., Portsmouth:
WRECKS OF SIX SISTERS AND OUR LADDIE HAVE BEEN REMOVED.

A cruiser was leading some destroyers on an operation against enemy coastal shipping. After much bad weather and no navigational fixes they found themselves not where they expected to be and almost certainly in a minefield.

From Cruiser to Flotilla Leader:
WHAT DO YOU CONSIDER IS OUR POSITION OTHER THAN PRECARIOUS.

Returning to Malta, after the bombardment of Catania, Sicily, on 17th July, 1943, H.M.S. *Warspite*, with paravanes streamed, made good 23½ knots in her thirtieth year.

From C.-in-C. Mediterranean to Flag Officer Force H:
OPERATION WELL CARRIED OUT. THERE IS NO QUESTION WHEN THE OLD LADY LIFTS HER SKIRTS SHE CAN RUN.

From Flag Officer, Gibraltar:
SMALL ROUND OBJECT SIGHTED 180 DEGREES 5 MILES FROM EUROPA POINT. PROBABLY MINE.

From Flag Officer Force H:
CERTAINLY NOT MINE.

H.M.S. *Ark Royal* on first emerging for sea trials *circa* 1938, passed another of H.M. ships.

From Ark Royal to passing ship:
HOW DO I LOOK.

Reply:
GO BACK TO LOCH NESS.

The British Pacific Fleet included a very small Rescue tug which tried hard but which could not keep up with the other ships during the assault on Japan. Commander-in-Chief's signal to Admiralty concerning this tug ended:

> . . . AM ORDERING HER TO RETURN TO BASE. I RECOMMEND STRONGLY SHE SHOULD SEEK FURTHER EMPLOYMENT ON THE THAMES BUT NOT BELOW TEDDINGTON LOCKS.

From Liverpool W/T Station to Admiralty:

> FOLLOWING RECEIVED FROM UNKNOWN SHIP. AM BEING INTERFERED WITH.

From Escort Leader to Corvette:

> THE DUCHESS OF RUTLAND IS SHOWING A DIM LIGHT LOW DOWN AMIDSHIPS.

Carrier joining Fleet after having been painted with new camouflage design receives following greeting from C.-in-C.:

> YOU LOOK LIKE A FREISIAN COW IN CALF.

After *Kelly* was torpedoed in the North Sea on 8th May, 1940, and again after *Javelin* was torpedoed in the Channel on 29th November, 1940, Captain Lord Louis Mountbatten, who was on board both these ships, made the same reply to the same signal from the next Senior Captain on each occasion.

Signal:

> IS CAPTAIN (D) ALIVE.

Reply:

> YES. YOU ARE NOT IN COMMAND OF THE FLOTILLA YET.

Following the brilliant Fleet Air Arm raid on Taranto.
From Flag Officer Force H to C.-in-C. Mediterranean:
CONGRATULATIONS ON SUCCESSFUL DE-BAGGING. IF THIS GOES
ON UNCLE BENITO WILL SOON BE SINGING ALTO IN THE CHOIR.

Senior Officer Atlantic convoy escort to rejoining corvette in
very bad weather:
WHY HAVE YOU TAKEN SO LONG TO REJOIN CONVOY.
Reply:
IT WAS UP HILL ALL THE WAY.

The troubles reported by Naval Officer in charge, Mersa
Matruh, when the port was first re-opened were as follows:
From Naval Officer i/c Mersa Matruh to Rear Admiral, Alexandria:
SOME GENIUS HAS SENT 1,000 AUSTRALIANS HERE. THEY ARE
SITTING ON THE PIER SHOUTING FOR FOOD. I HAVE NO FOOD,
NO SHIPS, NO STORES, NO TRANSPORT, NO INSTRUCTIONS, NO
REPLIES TO MY SIGNALS. SITUATION IS IMPOSSIBLE.
Reply from Rear Admiral, Alexandria:
DON'T LET THEM EAT YOU REPEAT YOU. HELP IS ON THE WAY.

From Corvette to C.-in-C. Plymouth:
ROMAN EMPEROR IN TOW BADLY DAMAGED PLEASE SEND TUGS.
From C.-in-C. Plymouth:
REVELATIONS CHAPTER 3 VERSE 11.[1]

From Senior Officer after inspecting small ship:
STANDING ORDERS PROVIDE FOR OVERALLS BEING WORN FOR
DIRTY WORK ON BOARD IN WHICH CATEGORY I DO NOT
INCLUDE AN INSPECTION BY ME.

---

[1] "Behold I come quickly: hold that fast which thou hast, that no man
take thy crown."

In 1937 H.M.S. *Cumberland* was returning from China with a collection of exhibits for the Chinese Ceramics Exhibition. On arrival at Portsmouth she made the customary signal to Commander-in-Chief Portsmouth.

REQUEST PERMISSION TO SALUTE YOUR FLAG.

C.-in-C. replied:

APPROVED, PROVIDED YOU DON'T BREAK THE CHINA.

Signal flying from destroyer as she emerges from a near miss.
PHEW.

During General Drill.
From Commander-in-Chief (Admiral Joe Kelly):

SEND BAND TO FLAGSHIP TO PLAY POPULAR TUNE. HAS ANYONE HERE SEEN KELLY IS NOT REPEAT NOT CONSIDERED A POPULAR TUNE.

From Tug towing battle practice target to firing cruiser whose shots are falling too close:

WE AIM TO PLEASE. YOU AIM TOO PLEASE.

From 1st Destroyer to 2nd Destroyer:
YOU HAVE A LIGHT SHOWING ON YOUR STOKERS MESS DECK.
Reply:
YOU ARE LOOKING ON TO MY STOKERS MESSDECK. HAVE JUST
BEEN IN COLLISION.

From Destroyer to unknown Trawler:
WHAT IS THE SIGNIFICANCE OF THAT SIGNAL YOU ARE FLYING.
From Trawler:
REGRET I DO NOT KNOW. FLAGS SMELT OF FISH.

From Protector to C.-in-C. Mediterranean:
EXPECT TO ARRIVE ALEXANDRIA 1600. HAVE 1,500 ITALIAN
PRISONERS ON BOARD, MIXED BUNCH RANGING FROM LIBYAN
SOLDIER AGED 10. ALL VERMINOUS.

From Base Routing Officer, Norfolk, Virginia to Admiralty:
LOUISE EJECTED FROM CONVOY KS529 FOR EXCESSIVE SMOKING.

From Base to Trooping Carrier:
CAN YOU FREIGHT 12 LIVE SOMALI SHEEP FROM ADEN TO
CEYLON.
Reply from Trooping Carrier:
SHIP WILL ONLY BE STOPPING OFF COLOMBO TO DISEMBARK
OFFICERS. CONSIDER IT WOULD BE INAPPROPRIATE TO LAND
SHEEP IN SAME BOAT.

From Terror (very old) to Protector off Sidi Barrani, 1941:
AM PROCEEDING AT FULL SPEED TO YOUR ASSISTANCE. MY
SPEED 4 KNOTS.

An aircraft was towing a drogue target down a line of cruisers who were firing at the target with A.A. armament. Suddenly a shell burst in front of the aircraft. The pilot immediately broadcast by Radio telephone:

I AM PULLING THIS BLOODY THING, NOT PUSHING IT.

R/T message from Free French pilot in Hurricane.

ENGINE NO GOOD. I JUMP.

A U.S. destroyer was ordered alongside a battleship at sea to fuel. She made several attempts to get into position but each time something went wrong and she sheered off and circled around for another try. When the Admiral commanding the Task Force could stand it no longer he signalled to the battleship:

SUGGEST YOU TRY GOING ALONGSIDE THE DESTROYER.

From U.S. Admiral Merrill, after leading his task force into action:

BOMBARDMENT FINISHED. TWO CRUISERS SUNK IN ADDITION. WHAT IS BAG LIMIT THIS YEAR ON THOSE BASTARDS.

Admiral Halsey replied:

THOROUGHLY PROUD OF YOUR BAG. IN THESE WATERS IT IS ALWAYS OPEN SEASON AND THE GAME WARDENS ARE ON VACATION. CONGRATULATIONS TO YOU AND YOUR GANG.

At Guadalcanal U.S. Intelligence learned that a Jap submarine would land a certain high official one night at Cape Esperance. Admiral Halsey's signal to the Commander of that area ended:

. . . IMPORTANT S.O.B. ABOARD. GET HIM.

Later the area commander replied:

SANK SUBMARINE. S.O.B. STILL ABOARD.

One winter H.M.S. *Sabre*, a destroyer, was alongside a dock-yard wharf under repair. She had no steam and only a few men on board. A gale blew which parted her lines and she charged helplessly across the harbour bouncing off anything in her path.

Eventually dockyard tugs appeared and took her firmly in hand. As they were bringing her back to her berth the only officer on board signalled to the resident Admiral:

STONE COLD SABRE.

After the spectacular Air strike on the Central Philippines in September, 1944, which accounted for 59 Jap ships and 478 of their planes, Admiral Halsey expressed his enthusiasm thus:

BECAUSE OF THE BRILLIANT PERFORMANCE MY GROUP OF STARS HAS JUST GIVEN I AM BOOKING YOU TO APPEAR BEFORE THE BEST AUDIENCE IN THE ASIATIC THEATRE.

The audience referred to proved to be Manila and when the Japs had been driven out Admiral Halsey said:

THE RECENT EXCEPTIONAL PERFORMANCE YIELDED GRATIFYING GATE RECEIPTS AND ALTHOUGH THE CAPACITY AUDIENCE HISSED VERY LOUDLY LITTLE WAS THROWN AT THE PLAYERS. AS LONG AS THE AUDIENCE HAS A SPOT LEFT TO HISS IN WE WILL STAY ON THE ROAD.

From U.S. Atlantic patrol aircraft:
SIGHTED SUB SANK SAME.